Modern History Through Canadian Eyes

A Canadian History Guide for All Ages

~Second Edition~

By Heather Penner

Solid Oak Publishing
www.solidoakpublishing.com

Solid Oak Publishing, Cold Lake, Alberta
www.solidoakpublishing.com

First Edition published by Solid Oak Publishing: 2005
Second Edition published by Solid Oak Publishing: 2007
Re-printed through Amazon: 2018

Library and Archives Canada Cataloguing in Publication

Penner, Heather, 1966-
        Modern history through Canadian eyes : a Canadian
history guide for all ages / by Heather Penner. -- 2nd ed.

Includes bibliographical references.

ISBN 9781980991861

        1. Canada--History--Study and teaching. I. Title.

FC57.P46 2007   971.0071   C2007-900639-6

Cover Photos: David Heaslip, July 1975, 'Ksan Historical Village, Hazelton, BC.
Heather Penner, August 2004, Fort Steele, BC.

Printed in Canada

Cover pictures

This picture is a little piece of history itself! It was taken by my father in July 1975 on a holiday trip my family took into northern BC. One of the stops on our trip was the 'Ksan Indian Village at Hazelton, BC, where we learned a great deal about the West Coast Natives and how they lived. I still remember the inside of this Fireweed House! The little girl in the yellow jacket is me, sitting beside my mother. My sister is standing in the foreground.

This series of pictures were all taken by me on a family holiday into southern BC in August 2004. They were taken at Fort Steele where we experienced what life was like in the 1880s. We rode on the steam train and that is my family in the horse-drawn wagon. The children enjoyed looking around the yard of this Scandinavian house, which was built by hand with incredible workmanship. By far our favourite part of the visit, however, was seeing the actors in the streets of the town, playing a role to make us feel like we really were in 1885! We went into the school house and were taught by the "teacher." We later saw a temperance demonstration on the front steps of the local hotel, during which some rather surprising events occurred that led us all to the court house to play a part in the outcome of these events. What an exciting way to learn about Canadian History!

Acknowledgements

My heartfelt thanks go first to my dear husband, Victor, who has supported me through the writing of two editions of this volume. He is my computer genius, honest critic, and most valued encourager. I am grateful for his calm and capable trouble shooting and problem solving when computer glitches and software idiosyncrasies had me tearing out my hair!

Thank you to Victoria, Matthew, Kathleen and Emily, who daily endure their mother's love of history, and have tested many of the ideas presented in this book.

Thank you to my parents for being my cheering section throughout the process, and who provided the vintage photograph of me, my mother and sister in front of the Fireweed House at 'Ksan Indian Village for the front cover.

Thank you to Angie Blackman, editor of Homeschooling Horizons Magazine, who continues to meet my myriad of e-mail questions with cheerful and willing advice, and whose vast experience has helped me over the many hurdles of publishing. Thanks again to the readers of Homeschooling Horizons whose enthusiastic response to the Canadian History articles gave a reason for this project, and to those whose appreciation for the first edition has encouraged me to make this second edition bigger and better.

And with the publishing of this second edition I owe a great deal to Rita Davidson, who gave freely and enthusiastically of her experience in printing advice, creative and marketing ideas, as well as valuable time and effort in designing this new and updated cover. I love it!

TABLE OF CONTENTS

Preface

In this expanded Second Edition of <u>Modern History Through Canadian Eyes</u> you will find even more resources than before, including one of my favourites: <u>A History of the English Speaking Peoples</u> by Winston Churchill. I hope you will find some favourites that will become treasures in your home library.

Because I am well acquainted with the limited time most homeschool parents and teachers have to prepare curriculum, I have included in this edition a planning chart to help make your preparation easier. The example given is just that: an example. These are the books I might use, but you may choose a completely different combination of resources. Once you have chosen your main resources, filling out these forms from the information in the guide should be a simple task. Feel free to photocopy as many of these blank forms as you need for your personal use with your family.

We all like to know what our children have remembered from their reading, so to help us assess this while keeping learning fun and non-intimidating, I have created some crossword puzzles for the students to do. Some are more challenging than others, so choose according to the students' abilities. If your students do not like doing crosswords, please do not force them to do these! There are many ways to assess knowledge, including oral discussion and many of the projects suggested in this guide.

I am also proud to include in this edition some samples of projects created by my own children in our study of Canadian History (pages 115 and 121). I hope these inspire you and your children to create you own unique projects.

My only "rule" is that you do not feel bound to this book. It is my belief that every curriculum plan should be as individual as each student is. Use this guide as a **guide**. Choose from it the resources that you can find. Add others that are not included. Choose projects that appeal to your family, or use my project ideas as a springboard for your own. Above all, enjoy your journey through Canadian History!

INTRODUCTION

Have you ever heard someone say they hate history - that history is boring? If you talk to them long enough you will probably discover the reason: They were made to memorize lengthy lists of names and dates which held no meaning for them other than as an item in a list, and the teacher called it "history." It is a sad death history has died for these unfortunate students. History, however, is not a list of faceless names. History is people and the lives they lived, sometimes not so different from our own. When we study history properly, we get to know these people. We imagine what life was like for them just as we do when reading a good work of fiction. With some knowledge of history, however, we can do more than imagine!

On a recent visit to my parents I had the chance to do this as I held a piece of history in my hands. My mother, knowing of my love of "old things," showed me a pocket size Bible she had found among my grandmother's belongings. Printed in 1854, most exciting to me was the inscription in faint but still readable beautiful Victorian script:

> *John T.* (we couldn't quite make out the last name)
> *From Mother*
> *September 26, 1857*
> *"Search the Scriptures„*

(Notice the quotation marks, which I assume are according to 1857 convention.)

My heart skipped a few beats as I held that book in my hands and imagined the mother who had lovingly penned those words in this gift for her son. I wondered how much John T. read his gift. Did he know its Author? Was it given to him when he left home? Was he going off to war; or to find work; or was he getting married? Perhaps the Bible was given on the occasion of his graduation from university, or on his birthday, celebrating his passage into adulthood. Did he treasure the Book because it was a gift from his mother?

Ok, so I am an incurable romantic! But to hold a piece of history in my hands and to read words penned by a woman - probably a relative - 150 years ago is a rare treat, indeed. I am not likely to receive answers to any of my questions about John T. and his mother, but it is enough to hold their book and think of whom they might have been. I had a similar feeling when I stood on the step of the Parliament Building in Ottawa, and thought of the great men who had stood there before me – on that very spot! I touched the words from Psalm 72:8 inscribed in the pillar, "He shall have dominion from sea to sea." Ah…history. History in its most real and alive form! History ought to be experienced whether through an artifact, a field trip, a novel, or a textbook.

It is my hope that in this guide to Canadian History you will find something intriguing in each unit – something that makes you long to know more. History is all about who came before us and how they changed the way things are. It is knowing where we've been so that we see more clearly where we are and where we are going. It reminds us of the mistakes of the past so that we might not repeat them in the future. It is a study of people, of places, of customs and hardship. It tells us that we belong to this land, and the land belongs to us. It reminds us that we owe our forefathers much for their cultivation and settlement of the land, and their development of law and order in our land. I hope you will find this study as interesting as I do. And I hope it leaves you, as it has always left me, longing to know more.

Planning

This guide should not be followed strictly as it is written. In fact, it is specifically designed to be molded to your own course of study, to meet the very individual needs of your family. Before you begin, look on your bookshelves and check out your local library. Make a list of all the books that you want to use in this study. Then simply insert each resource into the appropriate unit. Use my lists as guides to help you find more resources where your own are lacking, but never feel that you must use every resource listed, or that you must limit yourself only to those items on my lists.

One consideration when choosing resources will of course be the ages and reading levels of your children. I have tried to include materials in this guide for all ages, from primary to high school. Choose the ones that will interest your children. Not all of the books hold to strictly the same order when relating events in Canada's past, which sometimes made the compilation of these resources a challenge. However, I have done my best to include the material in the appropriate unit so that if you have students of various ages studying together, they will, for the most part, study the same events and people at the same time, even though their materials may differ. This should help you in planning field trips and other activities, as well facilitating the use of materials that will appeal to all ages, such as the video series, Canada: A People's History. Your children will also be enriched in their knowledge as they listen to your discussions with your other children, even if those discussions are above or below their level of complete understanding.

The key to coordinating your own resources is thinking chronologically. Read main resources (those covering a large time period) a chapter or section at a time, all the while thinking of your other books (or making notes) and how they will fit together. To simplify this, first choose which book will be your Main Resource (or spine). I have chosen The Story of Canada, by Janet Lunn. So as I planned, I first read one chapter in The Story of Canada. I jotted down notes about what time period is covered in that chapter. I wrote down Canadian events of that time period, as well as world events. Then I went through all my other resources that might have some information about this time period, drawing out from them any pages that could be useful in our study of that one chapter from my Main Resource. Don't forget those resources that cover world events that you want to study in conjunction with Canadian History.

For example, the first chapter in <u>The Story of Canada</u> is about the Natives of North America, how they came to North America, how they lived, various tribes, etc. After reading that chapter, I pulled out all my books that had anything to do with Native North Americans, and scanned them, jotting down any relevant pages. Once these resources were all coordinated, I began searching for literature. I chose books to read aloud with my children, as well as books at various reading levels for them to read on their own. These were then slotted into the appropriate time period under the heading, "Additional Reading."

At this point, supplementary resources can be added if you have access to videos or field trips pertaining to the time period to be studied. For example, if you live in Ottawa, schedule a trip to the Canadian War Museum when you reach the 1900's and begin your study of WWI. Plan a trip to Upper Canada Village during your study of the settlers of the late 1800's. Many towns across Canada have historical sites, museums or forts that can add a wonderful "hands on" element to your studies. The Home Works Guides are very good at listing some of the major locations, but you may be surprised at what good local research will uncover. If you have access to the internet, you will find many more resources and field trip ideas. Many sites you are unable to visit have virtual tours and information on-line.

If you are creative, be sure to add craft-type projects to your curriculum as well. The more kids can "do" in addition to "reading" and "hearing," the more they will remember from their studies. So add projects as your time and creativity allow. Why not paint a colourful picture of a totem pole when you study the Pacific Coast Natives? Better yet, use an empty paper towel tube and make a three-dimensional totem pole! Use paper maché or construction paper for the protruding parts. You are limited only by your own imagination! Do as many projects as you want, or skip the projects altogether. It is entirely up to you, the teacher.

I am no artist. Nevertheless, I have filled this guide with my own sketches of historical characters and events in the hope that I will encourage you and your students to try their hand at some of these types of projects. Some sketches are free hand, but for many I traced the outline first, and then filled in the details. (See if you can recognize all the portraits!) A great project would be to make a poster for a certain decade, showing what you believe the most significant events of that decade to be. (See my daughter's examples on pages 115 and 121.) And don't shy away from sketching people. Even if the end result isn't perfect, once you have attempted to draw a prime minister, you will never forget what he looks like! Surrounding his picture with symbols of the events that occurred during his years in power (as I did with Mackenzie King and others) will help solidify for the student the time he was prime minister, and the events/issues he had to deal with.

Don't forget writing projects as well, if you want to incorporate that into your history studies. Write a poem about a certain event, retell an event from the perspective of one of the characters involved, or get creative and make a video or a newspaper story about an event. Again, do as much of this as you have time and inclination for, or if you prefer, skip these kinds of projects all together. I have listed some suggestions for various types of projects in each unit, but please do not restrict yourself to my imagination! Watch for the interest of your children, and give them the freedom to delve deeper into the areas they enjoy, doing projects and activities that suit their talents and interests.

Now, go ahead and take those Canadian resources off your shelves! I have given you ideas for your own studies. Please realize, however, that my ideas are just that - my ideas! You can take the books you already have and use them just as I have used mine. Scour your library and discover what they have available for you to use. Pick up used books whenever you can. But don't feel you have to have any particular book just because I have used it here. This guide is not intended to be a complete History Curriculum, but merely a starting point that I hope will inspire you as you create your own personalized Canadian History program! Remember this is your program. Make it work for you!

World Connection

I have included in each unit a section called "World Connection" which suggests some possible research questions and projects intended to get older children thinking about how Canada fits into the context of the world of a particular time period. Younger children may not be able to make the associations on their own, but might begin to see their country in its world context if you help make those connections for them. Adapt these ideas to suit the ages and interests of your children.

Scheduling

How long you choose to spend on each unit is entirely up to you. Much will depend on how many hands on projects you do, how many hours per week you spend on Canadian History, and how in-depth you want your studies to be. I have basically followed the division of the chapters in The Story of Canada, by Janet Lunn. There are 10 chapters in this book, so you could easily spend one month on each chapter. Or you could use the chapter divisions in My First History of Canada, by Donalda Dicki, of which there are 21, and spend one week on each chapter. Choose whatever method will accomplish your goals for the study, and be flexible. There may be units that you skim through quickly, and others that you want to linger on. Feel free to follow your interests and make this study one you and your children will not only learn from, but enjoy.   I prefer to slow down our study as we approach the 20th Century.

I would encourage you to throw out the calendar as you plan your Canadian History studies! Ok, you can keep your calendar, but rather than making sure to be finished by a certain goal month, take your time in the study, spending as much time on each unit as you need to become familiar with the people, places, and events. There are plenty of resources listed here, and many more available from your library, book store, and used book resources. Take the time to meet the men and women who had a vision for a new country, those who rose to defend her, and those who struggled in her beginnings. Spend time doing hands-on projects so your children will be able to experience the time period, rather than only reading about it. They will remember so much more when activities and field trips are involved!

To help with your planning, I have divided the units into sections. I suggest at least a week for each section to study it thoroughly. Because the subject matter overlaps somewhat, I have included only one "projects" section and one "world connection" section at the end (with the exception of Unit 2). Fit these and other ideas of your own, wherever they fit into your study of each unit.

With each unit I try to choose one or two books for our read aloud time after lunch. For example, for Unit 2 I chose <u>And Tomorrow the Stars: The Story of John Cabot</u>, by Kay Hill.   Choose whatever book suits your family's interests.

Resources

Following is the list of resources for use in our study of Canadian History. Some are books I picked up at used book fairs and may not be easy to obtain. Others I found at the library. Nevertheless, use whatever you have available. I have given a brief review of the main resources in this guide to help you decide which books might be right for you. Check out as many of the books as you can yourself, though, because you may not agree with my evaluations. Most can be found in the library, allowing you several weeks to read the book and decide if you wish to purchase it. I have included which edition I used for this guide. Other editions are fine, but their page numbers may not correspond exactly with this guide.

I strongly recommend using more than one book as your core resource. There are vast differences in opinion and interpretation between the various authors listed here, which may not be obvious when reading just one or two. Reading one resource lays the foundation for your study. Reading a second adds another layer to your knowledge, colouring it in just a little. A third and fourth resource add more depth and dimension to the study, eventually creating a picture of past events that is more than just a list of facts. The more layers you add to your picture, the more accurate your knowledge will be, and the more interesting your study! Your goal should be to understand the events as closely as possible to having actually been there. If it is too much for your younger children to use more than one core resource, take the time to read several yourself so that your own knowledge will be well rounded and you will be aware of opinions in your core resource that may not be as authoritative as you may have thought had you read nothing else.

One common tendency among the various resources is to judge a person for an act or decision based on the outcome of that act or decision. While it is important to evaluate the outcome of decisions, it is also important to look at the information the decision-maker had available. Given the information available at the time, it may have been a wise decision, even though it did not turn out as expected. On the other hand, a person may have made a poor decision that turned out better than one would expect. Evaluate both the wisdom of the decision at the time, as well as the result, in fairness to the historical character, with discernment as to whether the character was in error, or simply unable to predict the future.

I recommend the Home Works Canadian History guides. In them you will not only find ideas for many questions and projects, but a wealth of background information on each part of Canada's History. I have not included it in the resource list because the chapters obviously correspond to those in The Story of Canada and in this guide.

Canadian History

The Story of Canada (Janet Lunn) 1996 Paperback Edition

This is a very popular book for teaching Canadian history, and for good reason. It is written in narrative form, with sidebars for extra events the author wished to highlight. The illustrations by Alan Daniel are beautiful and add interest to the text. I have used this book to form the outline for this study.

Two chapters seem out of place, chronologically, but it gives one the ability to thoroughly understand what is going on in the heart of Canada before moving westward. If you prefer to use one of the other texts as your base, simply omit units 5 and 6. If you are using The Story of Canada along with another text, you will have to either read chapters 5 and 6 when you come to them, leaving your other text aside to do so, or take the individual sections of these two chapters and insert them with the readings for the appropriate time period. For example, Chapter 5 begins with a section on the Plains Indians: Read that with Unit 1. The next section discusses the Fur Traders as they pushed westward: Read this section along with the Voyageur section of Unit 3, or along with the concurrent time period (late 1700s) of Unit 4. It may take some work to fit those two chapters in chronologically, and therefore be easier just to read them when you come to them, leaving aside your other studies for a time to concentrate on the discovery and settlement of the west.

This book makes a nice read-aloud, but can easily be read by students in middle school and above. The closer the book moves towards modern times, the more the author's personal views show through the text. Be aware of this so you can guide your students to understand where opinion is stated as fact, or where facts may not be entirely accurate due to a certain point of view. This book also contains evolutionary content at the beginning.

My First History of Canada (Donalda Dickie) 2002 Paperback Edition

As suggested by the title, this is a good first book in the study of Canadian History. It is geared to the youngest audience of any of the books, and is quite able to hold the attention of even primary age students. It makes a delightful read-aloud, but can easily be read by students as young as 8 and 9 – younger if they are good readers. There is a list of questions for each chapter at the back of the book to check for comprehension. This book also contains evolutionary content at the beginning.

The Spirit of Canada – 1999 Paperback Edition

This is one of my favourite books, showing Canadian History from a cultural perspective. It is filled with stories, myths, legends, poems, and songs, written throughout the ages of Canadian History.

Along with the entries, it gives a brief background surrounding each composition, including who wrote it, what their circumstances were, etc. This adds a real element of "being there" to our study, and helps us to understand the times we study more personally and thoroughly. Also included in the book are many entries "Just for Laughs."

The bottom line for all entries in this book is that they are 100% Canadian! Even better - my children love to take this book to the living room and curl up to read the many interesting stories found in it. That's the best recommendation any book could receive!

Footprints in the Snow (Robert Livesey)

What a charming title for a book about the men and women who have left their footprints on the history of our snowy northern country! This book contains synopses of the lives of over 75 Canadians, from athletes and authors of note to war heroes and politicians, all arranged in chronological order. Each chapter gives questions about the life of the individual studied. It is easy to read and is suitable for high school or even an interested middle school student. Unfortunately, this book is no longer in print, but I highly recommend searching used book resources and libraries for a copy.

Discovering Canada Series (by Robert Livesey)

This is an excellent series of books for children in primary and middle school. There is a lot of information given in an easy-to-read style, plus hands-on activities in each chapter. The crossword puzzles at the end of each book are a fun way to review the material. These books will appeal to those who want to move away from textbooks, but work well for those comfortable with a more traditional approach as well. Children love the activities included and I, for one, appreciate not having to come up with those activities on my own!

The series includes the following titles, many of which are referred to in this guide:

> Native Peoples
> The Vikings
> Fur Traders
> New France
> The Defenders
> The Railways
> The Loyal Refugees
> The Rebels

Kids' Book of Canadian History

This is neither a text nor a narrative, but is a good source of quick information in an easy to locate style. Strictly a supplementary resource, this is something that even young children can browse and receive a quick review of what they read in the other books. It is not likely to interest older students.

Each period of time is displayed on a 2 – 4 page spread and is full of pictures and short write ups describing various events and people.

This book is part of a series. All the books are laid out in the same format, and all can be used at some point during this study, if you like them. Several are used in this guide.

Kids' Book of Canada
Kids' Book of Canadian Prime Ministers
Kids' Book of Canadian Firsts
Kids' Book of the Far North
Kids' Book of the Canadian Railroad

Spotlight Canada (J. Bradley Curxton and W. Douglas Wilson) Third Edition

By far the most detailed of the resource books presented here, I found this book hard to put down! It is written in a very easy-to-read style, and could be used as young as middle school. Some content could be too much for younger readers, however (such as descriptions of WWI battles) so use discretion with those sections. For high school, however, this is an excellent text. It begins with confederation; so another resource is needed for the pre-confederation history of Canada.

Each chapter contains assignments which range from comprehension questions to deeper thinking questions, and includes a skill-building assignment for each section. Examples of this are note taking skills, mind mapping, using timelines, etc. For those who like to tie subjects together, this is a great way to use your History lessons to learn Language Arts skills.

This is definitely a textbook in design, so if you want to stay away from that format this would not be the book for you. Be aware, however, that you will miss a good deal of information that is not included in the narrative approaches that I have found. The fourth edition has been changed some, so if possible I recommend looking for a copy of the third edition.

A Short History of Canada (Desmond Morton) – 5th Edition

This is by far the best Canadian History book for high school students. It is concise, yet thorough, delving into the events of our country's past in more detail than any other resource listed. The author's views are kept in check as he presents a balanced account of Canadian History. This is also one of the most recent resources, and covers our history right up to the year 2000. I highly recommend this resource.

Canadian History for Dummies

As the title suggests, this book is written for today's fast food generation. It is easy to read and lighthearted, even irreverent at times. At the end of each section you will find a list to summarize what you just read, and many paragraphs have thematic icons in the margin so you'll know at a glance what you are reading. I have included this book mainly because the author presents a different point of view on some issues, which is important to explore. As always, watch for discrepancies between this and other resources.

The reading level of this book is roughly middle school level, but watch for a few unacceptable words if you are using it with younger children. It falls somewhere between a narrative and a textbook – it is laid out in a textbook style, but the writing is much more conversational than typical textbooks. Since this book is entertaining and easy to read it may be most appealing to the reluctant history student.

<u>Canada: A People's History (CBC video series)</u>

Videos are a great way to reinforce what has been read, or to introduce new material to your students. Videos also enable the student to picture what life was like during the events they are studying – how the people dressed, how they spoke, etc. These particular videos use original documents as the text spoken by historical characters, so the student hears the information first hand in the language of the day. The producers took care not to show too much violence, but some scenes or subjects may be too intense for younger viewers. As always, use discretion with your own children.

The videos are not organized in quite the same way as this study, so you might find you have to jump ahead or go back. I do not know that these are available on DVD, but if they are, viewing them would be easier. With the videos, just watch the titles as they appear and follow the guide for the unit you are studying. Of course, there is also the option of watching an entire video through during the most relevant unit. Use these in whatever way seems most logical to you.

World History

<u>The Story of the World (Susan Wise Bauer)</u>

This book is exactly what the title says it is - the story of the world. The author has a wonderful ability to tell a story and captivated my primary and middle school age children on the very first page. It makes a delightful read aloud, but could be read by any child old enough to read well. Older children (high school age) may find it too young for their liking.

There are four volumes in this set, the third and fourth dealing with the time period covered in this guide. (The first two are for ancient times and the Middle Ages.) Volume 3 covers the time period from the end of the Renaissance until the California gold rush in 1849. Volume 4 carries on from 1850 and takes the reader through to the end of the 20th century.

There is also a companion activity book available, which you may find helpful. It contains questions, colouring pages, puzzles and activities geared for the lower to middle elementary grades.

<u>A History of the English Speaking Peoples (Winston Churchill) 1958 edition</u>

If I could have Sir Winston Churchill over for tea, I would imagine him sitting in my living room holding his teacup, pinky politely poised, ready to discuss deeply complex topics of world import. What should I ask this learned gentleman? I think it would be most interesting to ask him to tell me a story. And what better story than the story of the western world?

This four-volume set is exactly what I imagine the story would sound like if Mr. Churchill were sitting in my living room telling me about the history of the English speaking peoples. These books give an insightful look at subjects that are often over simplified by our modern commentators and textbooks. The perspective is broad and encompasses the beliefs and feelings of those on every side of each situation, as well as facts that have long since been omitted from popular knowledge. I highly recommend this resource for high school students who wish to truly understand the world they live in, and to learn how to properly interpret the events of the world, past and present. It can be difficult to find, but it will be well worth the effort! Check your library and used book resources such as ebay.

Young People's Story of Our Heritage: The Modern World (V.M. Hillyer) 1966 edition

There are several volumes in this set, which would add to any study of World History of any era. The Modern World is the volume that is relevant to this study. This book provides an overview of each era from the 15th to the 20th century, with more detail for the more recent periods. It is in narrative format and easy to understand, making it ideal for middle school or early high school children, or perhaps older high school students who are not interested in the depth of study provided in Winston Churchill's books. I like the simple illustrations, mixed with photos and maps that add a visual component to the text without being flashy or distracting.

Usborne World History: The Last 500 Years

In typical Usborne style, this book contains brief accounts of events of the last 500 years. Events are displayed on a 2-page spread, organized chronologically and geographically, in colourful drawings and short text boxes.

Students will not glean a lot of information from this book, but it is a good supplementary reference for younger children who want to flip through an interesting book for quick tidbits: a good way to review what the child has already read or learned.

Invitation to the Classics (Louise Cowan and Os Guinness) 1998 edition

This book is a chronological review of great works of western literature and the men and women who penned them. It is excellent for those who want to include literature in their study of history, but are not well versed in the subject. I have listed some authors covered in this book with the appropriate units, but I leave the choice of which of each author's work to read up to you.

A First Book in American History (Edward Eggleston) 2000 edition

In similar style to My First History of Canada, this book is written for the lower elementary ages. Its format is somewhat like an old-fashioned reader, but it would also work well as a read aloud. Organized chronologically, it focuses on the lives of 18 historical American figures. Originally published in 1889, some of the text reflects the ideas of that era, including some terms that may now seem politically incorrect, and even derogatory. Taken in its historical context, however, children can learn that times and attitudes have changed, while learning about the people who lived during times that were different from our own.

Another book by the same author, <u>A History of the United States and Its People</u>, would be a better choice for slightly older students. I have not seen this book myself, but it is described as being geared towards ages 8-12.

Atlases

Maps are a wonderful aid in the study of history. I am a visual person, and find having a map open while I read about events of the past really helps me understand what has happened. It is not necessary for you to use the maps that I chose, but I highly recommend that you find a historical atlas that you like to use along with your study. I have included the map titles in this guide to make it easier for you to find similar maps in your own atlas, if you are using one other than the one I used.

The historical world atlas I used is a four-volume set called <u>World Atlas of the Past</u>, by John Haywood, published by Oxford University Press. There is quite a bit of text in this set, with a two-page write up, including pictures, for every two-page map.

For Canadian maps, I used <u>The Concise Historical Atlas of Canada</u>. Don't let the title fool you, though. At 11" x 15" and with 179 pages, this hardcover book is well over an inch thick! It is quite pricey, but you should be able to request it at your local library. It is called the "concise" atlas because it is the condensed version of a three volume set, which I have not seen but am sure is fantastic! In the Concise Atlas you will find maps relevant to every aspect of Canadian history; maps of exploration, population, and political territories for various time periods. Maps showing the history of highways and air travel in Canada, Native land use, religion, and libraries are also included. Each two-page spread shows maps of the same information for different years. Of course, there are also maps showing where battles were fought in the domestic wars in our past, as well as those showing the coming of the loyalists, the expulsion of the Acadians, and transatlantic migrations over the past two centuries. There are maps and graphs that show the various effects of the Great Depression, as well as world maps showing where Canadian forces fought in the World Wars. If you can afford this book, or can find it at your library, you will not be disappointed!

I have included every plate in the Atlas of Canada in this guide so that you will easily be able to choose which ones you would like to refer to for each unit. Do not feel you need to use them all. Again, I have included the plate titles to make your selection easier.

Other Resources

Military History of Canada: From Champlain to Kosovo (Desmond Morton)

This book would be of great value for the higher grades, or for yourself to read so that you can broaden the base from which you teach younger children. Of course if you or one of your students is particularly interested in military history, this is the book for you! However, even if that is not a special interest, this book gives a good solid history of our country. In fact, it is required reading by officers in the Canadian Forces. The military history of any country is intricately intertwined with its political history. Both are essential for a full understanding of where the country has come from. This resource is a bit more advanced than some of the other books listed, but an interesting read, nonetheless.

Who Killed Canadian History (J.L. Granatstein)

I am including this book not as a suggestion for curriculum, but as a good reference book for you, the teacher. J.L. Granatstein has been a university Professor of Canadian History for over 30 years. In this book he discusses the lack of good Canadian History curriculum in Canadian public schools and universities. He goes to great length to explain what the purpose of studying Canadian History is and what a good curriculum, in his opinion, would look like. I highly recommend this book for anyone who teaches Canadian History. It has given me lots to think about concerning what I personally teach in this area, and how I present the material.

Our Canada magazine (published by Readers Digest)

This is a beautiful publication all about Canada. While it doesn't pertain specifically to history, it is a wonderful way to see the landscape across the nation, which can help further our understanding of history. The magazine is entirely reader-written, and is heavy on photographs. Each issue has a photograph from every province in the "Coast to Coast" section, recipes from various locations in "A Taste of Canada," and a special feature column, again with plenty of beautiful photographs, highlighting one of Canada's provinces or territories. In addition, there are numerous articles about life in various corners of the country - a holiday up north learning to mush, a weekend in an ice castle in Quebec, or stories of how holidays are celebrated around the country. Each issue also tells "The Way it Was" in a regular column which unites us with our past. Filled with readers' memories of years gone by, it may contain a story of a grandfather who was a lighthouse keeper in Nova Scotia; a grandmother who was the first woman to drive a car in Regina; or memories of growing up in a little town in northern BC that used to be owned by the mill. The stories are charming, the photography stunning. Learn more about this publication at **www.ourcanada.ca**.

Over Canada: An Aerial Adventure (Presented by Royal Bank Financial Group)

This is a tremendous pictorial tour of Canada! The photography in this book is simply breathtaking. It is a wonderful way to familiarize yourself and your students with the vastness and beauty of our country as you study its beginnings and development. There is a video by the same name, from which the pictures in the book were taken. Both are wonderful assets to any study of Canada.

Videos

Many videos exist depicting various times in our history. I have included some that I have come across and found to be useful from a historical perspective. Search your local library and video store and use whatever you can find that you think will be helpful. Of course, use discretion with younger children. When videos can be used, they add a realistic element to the study that cannot be found on the printed page.

Political Cartoons

Political Cartoons are a fun way to study the political events of an historical period. They give a window into what people at the time were thinking about the various issues you may study. I still remember having political cartoons on my high school history tests when we studied WWII. Explaining the people and situations surrounding an historical political cartoon is not as easy as one might think, and the ability to do so demonstrates a good understanding of the issues at hand. After reading (and explaining) some cartoons, have your children draw their own for any time period they have studied. I have listed some books in appropriate units that I found in my local library. Search your library and bookstores and use whatever you are able to find. Be sure to read the introductions. Many of these books have information about the time period covered, some even explain the cartoons specifically. Editorial and Political Cartooning also gives a history of editorial cartooning. Going back as far as the Greeks, Romans and the Middle Ages, this is a very interesting book. Since it focuses on the 20th Century, I have placed this book in Unit 8, "Laurier's Sunny Ways." It could, however, be read at any point as an introduction to editorial cartooning, especially by students who wish to try their hand at this art.

Web Resources

The internet is an excellent resource for almost any subject! Be sure to check the source when reading information on the internet, and balance opinions with what you know to be fact. I have listed several websites that I have found useful in this study.

❖ **www.hyperhistory.com/online_n2/History_n2/a.html** - A good resource for placing world events into Canadian History is an on-line time line, complete with write-ups and many links.

❖ **www.foodtimeline.org/** - Gives origin of foods, arranged by date, and links to recipes and histories. For example, there is a link to a page of food eaten by Christopher Columbus!

❖ **www.classical-homeschooling.org/history/index.html** - While the authorship of this page is American, there are links to some great resources for European History, American History, as well as the First Peoples of North America.

❖ **www.archives.ca/02/02012001_e.html** - Some serious reading on Aboriginal History if you want to dig further yourself, or with your older teens.

❖ **www.warmuseum.ca/cwm/militaryhistory_e.html** - If you can't visit the museum, be sure to check out this page of links to the histories of various conflicts that have affected Canadian History.

❖ **www.civilization.ca/resourcee.asp** - The Canadian Museum of Civilization offers historical resources for teachers on their website.

❖ **www.canadainfolink.ca/history.htm** - This site is loaded with links to articles of specific people and events in Canada's history.

❖ **www.civilization.ca/orch/www04f_e.html** - This site offers a comprehensive list of historic sites in Canada, both general and by region.

UNIT 1 - ABORIGINAL PEOPLES

I started this unit with a book about the Ice Age. Both "The Story of Canada" and "My First History of Canada" begin with an evolutionary view of how the First Peoples arrived in North America. Since we believe in a young earth timeline, much of what is told in the first pages of these books must be edited and explained. Therefore, before we began I chose to read with my children a book about those beginnings written from the perspective of a young earth and a literal global flood preceding the Ice Age. "The Great Ice Age" was a very interesting and easily understood resource for that purpose. Feel free to skip this book if you disagree with my understanding of the earth's beginnings.

It could be argued that this unit is not really a part of "Canadian" History. When North America was inhabited solely by the aboriginal people, the country of Canada did not exist. Nevertheless, it is beneficial to meet the people who lived here before the Europeans came, because their culture, and even their existence, had a great effect on how the nation of Canada began. That is the purpose of Canadian History, after all: to discover who Canadians are and why Canada is the way it is through learning about those who influenced its culture from the earliest beginnings up to the present.

Of course, it is also important to study the history of Europe prior to the time of the explorers so as to better understand those influences on the early North American settlement. There are many resources for studying the Middle Ages and the Renaissance in Europe, so I will leave that subject for other curricula. It is generally recommended that one study history chronologically from the beginning to the present, so I hope that before you begin this study you will already be familiar with early European History. Nevertheless, whatever you have studied thus far, you have decided now to move on to Canadian History. So let's begin with the earliest residents of this land that was to become Canada.

Canadian Events/People

First Peoples living in North America

World Events/People

This time period serves as an introduction to Canadian History. If you have been studying history chronologically, you will have already covered this period in Europe and elsewhere.

Core Resources

The Story of Canada
Chapter 1 – A Hundred Centuries

My First History of Canada
Chapter 1 – The People in the Story
       Part 1 – The Indians were the
       first Canadians.
       Part 2 – Glooscap: an Indian
       hero.

A Short History of Canada
Part I – Different Histories
       Chapter 1 – New Nation
       Chapter 2 – First Nations

Discovering Canada: Native Peoples

Canada: A Book of Maps (Edward Owen), p. 45-63

The Spirit of Canada
When the World was New, p. 2
How Two-Feather Was Saved from Loneliness, (Abenaki, Eastern) p. 3
Manabozho and the Maple Trees (Anishinabe/Ojibwa, Woodland) p. 5
How the Thunder Made Horses (Siksika/Blackfoot, Plains) p. 7
Scannah and the Beautiful Woman (Tsimshian, Coastal) p. 9

Canadian History for Dummies
Chapter 1 – First Nations

Concise Historical Atlas of Canada
Plate 1 – Environmental Change After 9000 BCE
Plate 2 – Native Cultural Sequences, 6th Century to European Contact
Plate 3 – Native Population and Subsistence, 17ty Century

Story of the World
*Read chapter 1 between Unit 1 and Unit 2. It introduces the time period and tells of Spain's excursions into South America.
Chapter 1 – A World of Empires
       The Holy Roman Empire
       The Riches of Spain

Canada: A People's History
Episode 1 – When the World Began (15,000 BC – 1800 AD)
     Introduction (Beothuks, Migration of First Peoples)
     Women and Men
     Vision Quest
     Running Across the Sky
     War

Additional Reading

Life in the Great Ice Age (Oard/Snellenberger)
Eyewitness: North American Indian
Kids' Book of Canadian History - pages 4-7
Kids' Book of the Far North - pages 26-31
Footprints in the Snow - Glooscap, p. 2
How They Lived in Canada series:
     Sea and Cedar (Northwest Coast Indians)
     People of the Trail (Northern Forest Indians)
     People of the Buffalo (Plains Indians)
     People of the Ice (Inuit)
     People of the Longhouse (Iroquois)
     The Red Ochre People (Beothucks)
     Riel's People (Metis)
Atlas of The North American Indian (Waldman, Carl)

Project Ideas

❖ There are many projects suggested in the Discovering Canada Series. These books are a great investment, and provide all the ideas I will be able to do in this unit!

❖ Find recipes on the internet and have a Canadian Indian meal.

❖ For a snack, build a teepee using pretzels and dried fruit strips.

❖ Act out your favourite story from the lesson.

❖ On a map of Canada, show where the different people groups lived (Woodland, Plains, Pacific Coast, etc) then add tribal names. (Discovering Canada: Native Peoples and Eyewitness: North American Indian both have maps showing this information.)

❖ Start a time line on which to add people and events through the study.

❖ Choose one of the groups of First Peoples (east coast, woodland, plains, etc.) and tell how their environment affected their lifestyle (type of housing, food, hunting methods, etc.)

UNIT 2 – A MEETING OF CULTURES

The earliest meetings between native North Americans and Europeans were sometimes friendly and sometimes hostile. But they were always interesting! These early meetings would set the stage for future relations between the two people groups, so it is important to understand how each meeting took place and what kind of relationship each began.

Part 1 - VIKINGS

Canadian Events/People

Vikings

World Events/People

The Vikings fall in the period of the Middle Ages. If you have already studied them during a study of the Middle Ages, just a cursory review will be sufficient for this study. If not, just keep in mind that they lived during the time of knights and castles and the feudal system. If you want a deeper study of the Middle Ages at this time, Greenleaf Press's Famous Men of the Middle Ages is a good place to start.

Core Resources

The Story of Canada
Ch. 2, page 24-26 – Strangers on the Coast

My First History of Canada
Ch. 1, part 3 – The white men came from Europe.

Discovering Canada: Vikings

The Spirit of Canada
Thrand and Abidith, p. 15

Canadian History for Dummies
Chapter 2 – First Contact, pages 33-38

The Story of the World
Chapter 2 – Protestant Rebellions
        The Dutch Revolt
        The Queen Without a Country
Chapter 3 – James, King of Two Countries
        James and His Enemies
        King James's Town

World Atlas of the Past
Volume 3, page 8-11 – The World by 1530

Canada: A People's History
Episode 1 – When the World Began
        Into the Unknown (Vikings)
        A Continent of Nations

Additional Reading

Leif the Lucky (d'Aulaire, Ingri)
Kids' Book of Canadian History, p. 8
Usborne Famous Lives, p. 116-117
Famous Men of the Middle Ages

Project Ideas

❖ There are many ideas in the Discovering Canada Vikings book.

❖ Research the findings at L'Anse aux Meadows, and find pictures.

❖ Describe life in the Newfoundland Viking Village, and draw pictures.

❖ Write a story about a girl or boy your age who lived in a Viking Village or who was part of the group who first settled in North America.

❖ Research who the Vikings were, where they came from, and how they lived.

World Connection

❖ How were the Vikings affecting Europe during this time?

❖ Why did they make less of an impact in North America?

Part 2 – CABOT AND CARTIER

Canadian Events/People

Explorers
John Cabot
Jacques Cartier

World Events/People

Leonardo DaVinci
Michelangelo
Niccolo Machiavelli
Erasmus
Protestant Reformation (1483-1546)
Christopher Columbus
King Henry VIII
Elizabethan Period
Shakespeare (1564-1616)

Core Resources

The Story of Canada
Chapter 2 – Strangers on the Coast

My First History of Canada,
Chapter 2 – How America Was Discovered Again (1400-1500)
     Part 1 – Some people thought that the earth was a globe.
     Part 2 – Christopher Columbus discovered America in 1492.
     Part 3 – John Cabot discovered Canada in 1497.
Chapter 3 – How White Men Came to Live in Canada (1500-1600)
     Part 1 – French fishermen found the way in.
     Part 2 – Jacques Cartier's men traded buttons for furs and drank down a
          spruce tree in 1534.
     Part 3 – Sir Humphrey Gilbert took Newfoundland for England in 1583.
     Part 4 – Sir Francis Drake took the west coast for England in 1579.

The Spirit of Canada
Hunting for Unicorns, p. 20
The Village That Stretched from Sea to Sea, p. 23
Chikabash and the Strangers, p. 24

Canadian History for Dummies
Chapter 2 – First Contact, p. 38-45
     p. 45-47 – Champlain
     p. 48-52 – Frobisher/Hudson
     p. 52-end – Newfoundland, Fishing

A History of the English Speaking Peoples – Vol. 2 The New World
Book IV Renaissance and Reformation
       Chapter 1 – The Round World
       Chapter 2 – The Tudor Dynasty
       Chapter 3 – King Henry VIII
       Chapter 4 – Cardinal Wolsey
       Chapter 5 – The Break with Rome
       Chapter 6 – The End of the Monasteries
       Chapter 7 – The Protestant Struggle
       Chapter 8 – Good Queen Bess
       Chapter 9 – The Spanish Armada
       Chapter 10 – Gloriana

Young People's Story of Our Heritage – The Modern World
       Introduction
       The Renaissance
       Age of Discovery – Columbus
       Explorers and Explorations
       The Search for Gold and Adventure
       Religious Reform
       England Gains Control of the Sea

Concise Historical Atlas of Canada
Plate 5 – Exploring the Atlantic Coast, 16th and 17th Centuries
Plate 6 – Exploration, 17th, 18th Centuries

A First Book in American History
Chapter 1 – The Early Life of Columbus
Chapter 2 – How Columbus Discovered America
Chapter 3 – Columbus After the Discovery of America
Chapter 4 – John Cabot and His Son Sebastian

World Atlas of the Past
Volume 3, pages 24-27 – The European Reformation

Canada: A People's History
Episode 1 – When the World Began
       First Contact
       New Lands (Columbus, Cabot)
       The Land God Gave to Cain (Cartier)
       Hochelaga
       A Star Was Lost in the Sky
Episode 2 – Adventurers and Mystics (1540-1670)
       (Martin Frobisher)
       The Lost Colony (Newfoundland)

Additional Reading

Columbus (d'Aulaire, Ingri)
Kids' Book of Canadian History, p. 9-11
Usborne Famous Lives, p. 118-119 (Columbus)
Usborne Famous Lives, p. 122 (Elizabeth I)
Usborne The Last 500 Years, p. 6-7 (Exploring the World)
Jacques Cartier, Samuel de Champlain and the Explorers of Canada (Coulter, Tony)
Masters of Art Series: Leonardo da Vinci (Romei)
Spy for the Night Rider (Jackson, Dave & Neta) - Martin Luther
Christopher Columbus: A Great Explorer (Greene, Carol)
And Tomorrow the Stars: The Story of John Cabot (Hill, Kay)
Cartier Sails the St. Lawrence (Averill, Esther)
Cartier, Finder of the St. Lawrence (Symes, R.)
The Bold Heart: Story of Father Lacombe (Josephine)
Coronation of Jane Seymour (Meroff, D.)
William of Orange - the Silent Prince (Van de Huslt)
Shakespeare's England: Life in Elizabethan & Jacobean Times (Pritchard, R.E.)
Any of Shakespeare's plays that you would like to study with your children. If your children are young, consider Charles and Mary Lamb's "Tales from Shakespeare"
Invitation to the Classics – Niccolo Machiavelli (p. 131-134)
Invitation to the Classics – John Calvin (p. 135-138)
Invitation to the Classics – William Shakespeare (p. 149-154)

Project Ideas

- ❖ Draw a map of a make-believe world.

- ❖ Imagine seeing a new land for the first time. Write a paragraph describing what you see.

- ❖ Learn about navigational tools used during Cartier's time.

- ❖ Learn how to use a sextant.

- ❖ Go to a park (preferably one with lots of paths) and plot the directions you travel by using a compass and a hand-drawn map.

- ❖ Go to an open field or a park that is well known to you. Plot directions using a compass and put a "treasure" at the end.   Have your children find the treasure using your directions.

- ❖ Go outside after dark on a clear night and see if you can find north, south, east and west using the stars for direction. Perhaps plan a treasure hunt similar to the above, using the stars for direction instead of a compass.

World Connection

- ❖ Why did the various explorers leave their safe home to venture into the unknown? What were they looking for? Did they find it?

- ❖ How did the new way of thinking during the Renaissance influence the exploration of the world?

- ❖ In what ways was Leonardo da Vinci like the explorers of his day?

- ❖ In the fight for territory, which country gained the most? Which countries won land by war? By exploration? By cooperation?

- ❖ Which country do you think went about expanding in the right way? The most effective way? Why?

UNIT 3 – CHAMPLAIN AND BEAVER PELTS

In the last unit we learned about the people who lived in North America before the Europeans came. We learned about the first Europeans to "discover," explore, and settle North America. This unit will look into the exciting lives of those who chose to live in this new world, and those who chose to explore it, taking us one step further toward the beginning of what we now call Canada.

Part 1 – SETTLEMENT

Canadian Events/People

Champlain
Jean de Brebeuf & the Jesuit priests
Henry Hudson

World Events/People

English Civil War (Cromwell/Charles I)
Pocohontas (1617)
Mayflower (1620)

Core Resources

The Story of Canada
Chapter 3, pages 46-49 – Habitants and Voyageurs
Pages 49-51 – The Corngrowers

My First History of Canada
Chapter 4 – At First Canada Was All French (1600-1612)
      Part 1 – Champlain reported on Canada.
      Part 2 – De Monts built Port Royal in 1605.
      Part 3 – Champlain built Quebec and fought the Iroquois.
      Part 4 – John Guy built Cupids and picnicked with the Beothuks in 1610.
      Part 5 – Henry Hudson discovered Hudson Bay in 1610.
Chapter 5 – The Settlers Worked Hard to Get a Start (1610-1642)
      Part 1 – Champlain laid out the fur trade trail to the west.
      Part 2 – The English took Acadia, but the French took her back.
      Part 3 – Quebec had the first church and school.
      Part 4 – Father Jogues was a hero.

A Short History of Canada
      Chapter 3 – Cartier's Quebec

Discovering Canada: New France
Ch. 1 "Father of New France"
Ch. 3 "The Giant Black Robe"

Chapter 9 – The Western War
        The Thirty Years' War, 1618-1648

Concise Historical Atlas of Canada
Plate 6 – Exploration, 17th, 18th Centuries
Plate 7 – Exploration from Hudson Bay, 18th Century
Plate 8 – Exploration in the Far Northwest, 18th and 19th Centuries

World Atlas of the Past
Volume 3, pages 16-19 – Colonial North America
Volume 3, pages 28-31 – Europe in Conflict

Canada: A People's History
Episode 1 – When the World Began
        Northwest Passage (Henry Hudson)

Canada: A People's History
Episode 2 – Adventurers and Mystics
        Champlain's Gamble (Tadoussac, Etienne Brule)
        The Price of Friendship (Hurons)
        A Frenchman Among the Hurons (Brule, Gabriel Dumont)
        A Precarious Colony
        Black Robes in the Dark Forest (Jesuit Missionaries)
        A Holy City in the Wilderness (Marie de L'Incarnation, Jeanne Mance)
        Death of a Nation (Hurons, Disease, Iroquois attacks)

Additional Reading

Kids' Book of Canadian History, "Meeting of Cultures," p. 12-14
Canada: Portraits of Faith, p. 17 (Jean de Brebeuf)
Footprints in the Snow, p. 10 (Jean de Brebeuf)
Forts of Canada, p. 12-13 (Forts of the Black Robes)
Time Traveller Book of New France (Wernick, Morris)
With Pipe, Paddle, and Song (Yates, Elizabeth)
Champlain, Father of New France (Edwards, C.P.)
When the Morning Came (Prins, Piet)
The First Canadian (Ritchie, C.)
Henry Hudson, Captain of the Icebound Seas (Carmer, Carl)
The King's Loon (Downie, Mary)
Shooshewan: Child of the Beothuk (Gale, Donald)
The Red Ochre People (Marshall, Ingeborg)
Pocahontas: Daughter of a Chief (Greene, Carol)
Pocahontas, True Princess (Hanes, Mari)
Mary of Plymouth (Otis, James)
Invitation to the Classics – Miguel de Cervantes (p. 139-142)
Invitation to the Classics – John Donne (p. 155-158)

Part 2 – THE COLONY

Canadian Events/People

English and French in Canada
Radisson & Groseillier
Lord Talon
Madeleine de Vercheres

World Events/People

John Bunyan (1628-1688)
Louis XIV (1638-1715)
Galileo, Kepler
Isaac Newton discovers gravity (1665)
Charles II
William of Orange (1650-1702)
Glorious Revolution (1688 England)

Core Resources

The Story of Canada
Pages 51-53 – Champlain's Colony
Pages 53-56 – Louis XIV Saves New France
Pages 56-60 – Habitants
Pages 61-65 –Voyageurs

My First History of Canada
Chapter 6 – Both English and French Colonies Had to Fight for Their Lives (1612-1660)
    Part 1 – The Newfoundlanders fought the pirates.
    Part 2 – The Acadians fought each other.
    Part 3 – Good women built a school and a hospital at Quebec.
    Part 4 – Ville Marie, the City of Mary.
    Part 5 – The Iroquois killed the Hurons.
    Part 6 – The heroes saved Canada.
Chapter 7 – Canada Began to Grow (1658-1672)
    Part 1 – Radisson and Groseilliers saved Canada's trade.
    Part 2 – Radisson and Groseilliers led the English to Hudson Bay.
    Part 3 – Talon set Canada on her feet.
    Part 4 – The good coureurs worked for Canada.
    Part 5 – The Newfoundlanders fought the fishing admirals.
    Part 6 – Newcomers in Newfoundland.

Discovering Canada: New France
Chapter 4 - The Battle at Long Sault
Chapter 5 - The Great Intendent
Chapter 7 - A Young Heroine

The Spirit of Canada
The King's Daughter, p. 30

Canadian History for Dummies
Chapter 4 – Life in New France
Chapter 5 – Fur Wars

A History of the English Speaking Peoples – Vol. 2 The New World
Book VI – The Restoration
      Chapter 19 – The English Republic
      Chapter 20 – The Lord Protector
      Chapter 21 – The Restoration
      Chapter 22 – The Merry Monarch
      Chapter 23 – The Popish Plot
      Chapter 24 – Whig and Tory
      Chapter 25 – The Catholic King
      Chapter 26 – The Revolution of 1688

Young People's Story of Our Heritage – The Modern World
      Rise of the French Monarchy

The Story of the World
Chapter 10 – Far East of Europe
      Japan's Isolation: Closed Doors in the East
      The "Foreign Conquest" of China: The Rise of the Manchu
Chapter 11 – The Moghul Emperors of India
      World Seizer, King of the World, and Conqueror of the World
      Aurangzeb's Three Decisions
Chapter 12 – Battle, Fire, and Plague in England
      Charles Loses His Head
      Cromwell's Protectorate
      Plague and Fire
Chapter 13 – The Sun King
      The Sun King of France
Chapter 14 – The Rise of Prussia
      Frederick, the First Prussian King
Chapter 15 – A New World in Conflict
      War Against the Colonies: King Philip's War
      War Against the Colonies: Louis XIV Saves France
      William Penn's Holy Experiment

Chapter 16 – The West
      The Universal Laws of Newton and Locke
      Scientific Farming

A First Book in American History
Chapter 11 – William Penn
Chapter 12 – King Philip
Chapter 13 – Captain Church in Philip's War
Chapter 14 – Bacon and His Men

Canada: A People's History
Episode 2 – Adventurers and Mystics
      Great Expectations (Iroquois attacks on New France)
      The King's Daughters (Jean Talon, Filles de Roi)
      Birth of the Canadiens (Settling the colony)
Episode 3 – Claiming the Wilderness (1670-1755)
      (La Salle, Courer de Bois, Frontenac, Louis XIV)
      The First Colonial War (Perot, French and English at war)
      The Great Peace (Peace between the Indians and the French)
      1749 Was a Very Good Year (Life in New France)
Episode 6 – The Pathfinders (1670-1850)
      (David Thompson, Radisson, Grosseillier, Hudson's Bay Company)
      The River Route (Pierre de la Verendryes)

Concise Historical Atlas of Canada
Plate 34 – The French Origins of the Canadian Population, 1608-1759
Plate 43 – Trade in Interior America, 1654-1666
Plate 47 – Acadian Marshland Settlement, 1671-1714
Plate 50 – The Countryside, New France, ca 1700
Plate 51 – The Towns, New France, 1685-1759
Plate 59 – Rupert's Land, From 1670

Additional Reading

Kids' Book of Canadian History, "New France," p. 15-17
Kids' Book of Canadian History, "Traders and Explorers," p. 18-20
Canada: Portraits of Faith, p. 22 (Jeanne Mance)
Canada: Portraits of Faith, p. 26 (Marguerite Bourgeoys)
Footprints in the Snow, p. 17 (Adam Dollard)
Footprints in the Snow, p. 12 (Pierre Radisson)
Footprints in the Snow, p. 15 (Madeleine de Vercheres)
Forts of Canada, p. 10-11 (Home Sweet Fort: The Habitations)
Usborne Famous Lives, p. 123 (William of Orange)
Traitor in the Tower (Jackson, Dave & Neta)
Pilgrim's Progress (Bunyan, John)
Captured by the Mohawks (North, Sterling)
Fur Trader of the North (Symes, R.)

Madeleine Takes Command
Pilgrim's Progress (Bunyan, John)
Invitation to the Classics – George Herbert (p. 159-162)
Invitation to the Classics – John Milton (p. 163-168)
Invitation to the Classics – Blaise Pascal (p. 169-172)
Invitation to the Classics – John Bunyon (p. 173-176)

Part 3 – ACADIA

Canadian Events/People

Acadian Expulsion (1755)

World Events/People

French-Indian War (7 Years' War)
Siege of Louisburg (1745)
Bach (1685-1750)
Handel (1685-1759)
Voltaire (1694-1778)
Rembrant
Peter the Great (Reigned 1682-1725)

Core Resources

The Story of Canada
Pages 66-68 – The Struggle for Acadia

My First History of Canada
Chapter 8 – Canada Spread North, West, and South (1670-1690)
      Part 1 – Talon took possession of the north and west.
      Part 2 – Jolliet explored the Mississippi River in 1673.
      Part 3 – Governor Frontenac made the Iroquois behave.
      Part 4 – La Salle took the south-west for Canada in 1682.
      Part 5 – The boy Kelsey discovered the prairies in 1690.
Chapter 9 – The French Canadians Fought the Iroquois and the English for Canada (1660-1700)
      Part 1 – The fight for Hudson Bay.
      Part 2 – The wasp's nest.
      Part 3 – The English won in Acadia in 1690.
      Part 4 – Frontenac saved Quebec for France.
      Part 5 – The story of Madeleine of Vercheres.

The Spirit of Canada
Mon Canot, p. 34
Turbulent Times, p. 48
Leaving Acadia, p. 49

Canadian History for Dummies
Chapter 6 – Acadia

A History of the English Speaking Peoples – Vol. 3 The Age of Revolution
Book VII – England's Advance to World Power
    Chapter 1 – William of Orange
    Chapter 2 – Continental War
    Chapter 3 – The Spanish Succession
    Chapter 4 – Marlborough: Blenheim and Ramillies
    Chapter 5 – Oudenarde and Malplaquet
    Chapter 6 – The Treaty of Utrecht

Young People's Story of Our Heritage – The Modern World
    Peter the Great of Russia
    Frederick the Great of Prussia

Concise Historical Atlas of Canada
Plate 35 – The Seven Years' War
Plate 36 – Acadian Deportation and Return, 1750-1803
Plate 48 – Maritime Canada, Late 18th Century
Plate 49 – Resettling the St. Lawrence Valley, 1608-1760
Plate 60 – Fur Trade in the Interior, 1760-1825

The Story of the World
Chapter 17 – Russia Looks West
    Peter the Great
    Peter's Port to the West
Chapter 18 – East and West Collide
    The Ottomans Look West - Twice

World Atlas of the Past
Volume 3, page 32-35 – The Age of Enlightenment
Volume 3, page 40-43 – The Expansion of Russia

Canada: A People's History
Episode 3 – Claiming the Wilderness
    The Oath (Acadia under English rule)
    The Great Dispersal (Acadian Expulsion)

Additional Reading

Calico Captive (Speares, Elizabeth)
Escape From Grand Pre (Thompson, Frances)
Invitation to the Classics – Jonathan Swift (p. 177-182)

Part 4 – WAR ON THE PLAINS OF ABRAHAM

Canadian Events/People

Wolfe and Montcalm

World Events/People

Haydn (1732-1809)
Frederick the Great (1712-1786)
Benjamin Franklin
Fahrenheit invents the Mercury Thermometer (1718)

Core Resources

The Story of Canada
Pages 68-75 – The War of the Conquest

My First History of Canada
Chapter 10 – Peace and War: Good Times and Hard Times (1700-1760)
      Part 1 – The Canadians enjoyed themselves.
      Part 2 – The Verendryes led Canada out across the prairies.
      Part 3 – The Newfoundlanders got a Governor.
      Part 4 – The English build Halifax.
      Part 5 – Governor Lawrence exiled the Acadians.
      Part 6 – How the British Won Canada

Discovering Canada: New France
Chapter 8 - The Plains of Abraham

The Spirit of Canada
The Piper's Refrain, p. 54
Brave Wolfe, p. 57

Canadian History for Dummies
Chapter 7 – The Conquest
Chapter 8 – Aftermath

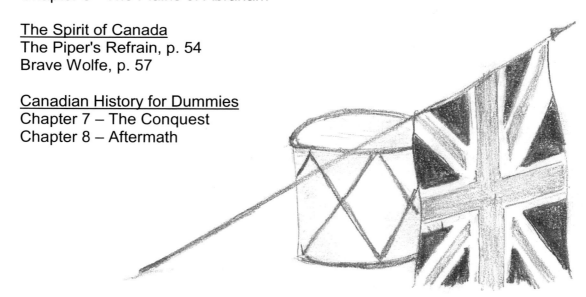

A History of the English Speaking Peoples – Vol. 3 The Age of Revolution
Book VIII – The First British Empire
      Chapter 7 – The House of Hanover
      Chapter 8 – Sir Robert Walpole
      Chapter 9 – The Austrian Succession and the "Forty-Five"
      Chapter 10 – The American Colonies
      Chapter 11 – The First World War

The Story of the World
Chapter 19 – The English in India
      The Indian Empire Falls Apart
      The Shopkeepers' Invasion
Chapter 20 – The Imperial East
      Emperor Chi'en-lung's Library
      The Land of the Dragon
Chapter 21 – Fighting Over North America
      Three Pointless Wars
      The Seven-Year War

A First Book in American History
Chapter 15 – Boyhood of Franklin
Chapter 17 – Franklin, The Printer
Chapter 18 – The Great Doctor Franklin

Canada: A People's History
Episode 4 – A Battle for a Continent (1754-1775)
      The Governor and the General (France and England at war, William Pitt)
      A Deterring and Dreadful Vengeance (Wolfe)
      The Inevitable Hour (Bouganville, John Knox)
      The River of Fire (British siege Quebec City)
      Divided Councils, Desperate Plans (George Townsend)
      The Plains of Abraham
      The Winter (Life after the war)
      Tide of Fortune (French attack Quebec City)
      Carving the Spoils (Pontiac, Small Pox)

Additional Reading

Kids' Book of Canadian History, "War!" p. 21-23
Footprints in the Snow, p. 22 (Montcalm and Wolfe)
Drummer Boy for Montcalm (Hayes, Wilma P.)
Wofgang Amadeus Mozart: Musician (Greene, Carol)
Medicine Maid: The Life Story of a Canadian Pioneer (Hoople, Elizabeth L.)
Streets of Gold (Rawlyk, G.)
A Proper Acadian (Downie, Mary)
Benjamin Franklin: A Man With Many Jobs (Greene, Carol)
Benjamin Franklin (D'Aulaire)

The Chimney Sweep's Ransom (Jackson, Dave & Neta)
Invitation to the Classics – Jonathan Edwards (p. 181-184)
Invitation to the Classics – Samuel Johnson and James Boswell (p. 185-189)
War in the 18th Century – History of Warfare Series (Westwell, Ian)
Wolfe & Montcalm: Their Lives, Their Times, And the Fate of a Continent
      (Carroll, Joy)

Project Ideas

❖ Consider researching food eaten by the habitants and/or voyageurs and have a camp out, cooking over an open fire as they would have.

❖ Take a canoe ride - a short ride if your children are little, or an overnight canoe trip with older children. Try a short portage to gain appreciation for the way the voyageurs had to travel! (You may have to postpone this for warmer weather! But don't let that stop you from doing it. Just relate it back to your studies in the spring.)

❖ If you know someone who knows a foreign language, try to communicate with him or her without using English. How easy is it? What do you have to do to understand each other?

World Connection

❖ How did the 7 Years' War in Europe affect those living in North America?

❖ Research the life one or more of the Europeans listed above.

❖ Listen to music written by J.S. Bach and Handel. Compare the styles. Listen to music by Haydn. How is it similar/different from Bach and Handel's music?

❖ Research the properties of mercury as it relates to its use in Fahrenheit's thermometer.

❖ How did the discoveries in astronomy and other sciences help those traveling to North America?

UNIT 4 – SETTLING THE COLONY

Not yet officially a country, Canada is beginning to take shape, nonetheless. In this unit we meet the colonists - the people who gave up the comforts of established society in Europe to brave the wilds of the new land across the

ocean! People like Catharine Parr Traill and her sister Susanna Moodie. Meet the men who began to establish towns in this new land. Military men like Col. John By who established ByTown, which later became Ottawa, and who dug the Rideau Canal with the help of his soldiers. Meet Big Joe Mufferaw, one of Canada's very own lumberjack legends!

Colourful people come to the forefront in Canada's history, and it is exciting to learn about them and their adventures. However, there is also war in Canada's history, and in this unit we will begin to see what Canada is about. We will see those loyal to the English throne flock to Canada to escape the rebels of the south. We will see those within Canada begin a rebellion of their own. And we will see the true grit of those early Canadians as they endure war with their closest neighbours. Beginnings usually bring exciting adventure due to the very newness of the experience. But the road is often fraught with hardship, and the success of the new venture often depends on those individuals willing to work hard toward that end. Canada's history is no exception.

Meanwhile, some important events were taking place in Europe. Take some time to learn about the French Revolution, beginning with the Storming of the Bastille in 1789. What caused the people to revolt? What were their grievances? What was life like for the various classes in that time? Find out how that revolution ended, and learn what kind of a man Napoleon was. Why was he able to gain power? What happened as a result of his being in power? How did his reign and the ensuing wars affect the other European countries? Once you have explored the Napoleonic era in Europe, put yourself back in Canada during that time. How would the world events have affected those living in the new world?

Part 1 – REFUGEES

Canadian Events/People

Loyalists come to Canada from the United States
Quebec is divided into Upper Canada and Lower Canada

World Events/People

Daniel Boone
Capt. Vancouver (1757-1798)
George Washington (1732-1799)
American Revolution (1763-1783)
Ludwig von Beethoven (1770-1827)
French Revolution (1789-1795)
Thomas Jefferson (1743-1826)

Core Resources

The Story of Canada
Chapter 4, pages 78-79 – The Colonists
Pages 79-84 – Refugees
Pages 84-86 – Gentlemen and Governors

My First History of Canada
Chapter 11 – The French and the English Got On Well Together (1763-1795)
        Part 1 – In Quebec they helped each other.
        Part 2 – The Governor called the Acadians home.
        Part 3 – French and British Canadians became partners in the fur trade.
        Part 4 – English sailors explored Canada's west coast.
Chapter 12 – The United Empire Loyalists Came to Canada (1775-1840)
        Part 1 – The English colonies became the United States.
        Part 2 – The Loyalists went to Nova Scotia and Prince Edward Island, and
                made the new province of New Brunswick.
        Part 3 – Governor Haldimand helped the Loyalists in Quebec.
        Part 4 – The Loyalists started Ontario.
        Part 5 – The Canadians began to govern themselves.

Canadian History for Dummies
Chapter 9 – Canada and the American Revolution

Concise Historical Atlas of Canada
Plate 12 – Eastern Canada, ca 1800
Plate 37 – The Coming of the Loyalists, Late 18th Century

A History of the English Speaking Peoples – Vol. 3 The Age of Revolution
Book VIII – The First British Empire
        Chapter 12 – The Quarrel With America
        Chapter 13 – The War of Independence
        Chapter 14 – The United States
        Chapter 15 – The Indian Empire
Book IX – Napoleon
        Chapter 16 – The Younger Pitt
        Chapter 17 – The American Constitution
        Chapter 18 – The French Revolution
        Chapter 19 – France Confronted

Young People's Story of Our Heritage – The Modern World
        The American Revolution
        The French Revolution

The Story of the World
Chapter 22 – Revolution!
        Discontent in the British Colonies
        The American Revolution
Chapter 23 – The New Country
        The American Constitution
        The First American President (1789-1797
Chapter 24 – Sailing South
        Captain Cook Reaches Botany Bay
        The Convict Settlement

A First Book in American History
Chapter 18 – Young George Washington
Chapter 19 – Washington in the French War
Chapter 20 – Washington in the Revolution
Chapter 21 – The Victory at Yorktown and Washington as President
Chapter 22 – Thomas Jefferson
Chapter 23 – Daniel Boone
Chapter 24 – Robert Fulton and the Steamboat

World Atlas of the Past
Volume 3, pages 20-23 – The American Revolution
Volume 3, pages 56-59 – The World by 1815

Canada: A People's History
Episode 4 – A Battle for a Continent
        The World Turned Upside Down (Canada is given to England, James
        Murray)
        The Quebec Act (Gen. Sir Guy Carlson, Boston Tea Party)

Episode 5 – A Question of Loyalties (1775-1815)
    (American Revolution, Loyalists, Thomas Walker)
    Invasion (Montgomery, Benedict Arnold, Invasion of Quebec)
    The Siege (Walker is killed, Arnold defeated)
    The World Turned Upside Down (Rebels and Loyalists)
    His Majesty's Loyal Allies (Joseph Brandt, Native role in the Revolution)
    Exile (British are defeated, loyalists flee to Nova Scotia)
    Nova Scotia (Loyalists settle Nova Scotia and New Brunswick)
    The Upper Country (Canada divided, Simcoe draws in Americans)

Additional Reading

Kids' Book of Canadian History, p. 24-27
Daniel Boone: Man of the Forest (Greene, Carol)
Captain of the Discovery (Haig-Brown, Roderick)
Vancouver, Explorer of the Pacific Coast (Syme, Ronald)
The Sky Caribou (Hamilton, Mary)
Warrior's Challenge (Jackson, Dave & Neta)
Beginning Again, Further Adventures of a Loyalist Family (Fryer, Mary Beacock)
Escape, Adventures of a Loyalist Family (Fryer, Mary Beacock)
And Then What Happened, Paul Revere? (Fritz, Jean)
Charlotte (Lunn, Janet)
Can't You Make Them Behave, King George? (D'Aulaire)
Flight (Crook, Connie)
Meyer's Creek (Crook, Connie)
George Washington (D'Aulaire)
George Washington's Mother (Fritz, Jean)
George Washington's Breakfast (Fritz, Jean)
Ludwig von Beethoven: Musical Pioneer (Greene, Carol)
Thieves of Tyburn Square (Jackson, Dave & Neta)
Why Don't You Get a Horse, Sam Adams? (Fritz, Jean)
Beethoven and the Classical Age (Bergamini, Andrea) (Masters of Music Series)
Invitation to the Classics – Jean-Jacques Rousseau (p. 195-198)
Invitation to the Classics – Alexander Hamilton, James Madison, and John Jay (p. 199-202)

Part 2 – WAR OF 1812

Canadian Events/People

The War of 1812

World Events/People

Elizabeth Fry (1780-1845)
Reign of Napoleon (1804-1814)
Napoleonic Wars (1795-1815)
Jaques-Louis David

Core Resources

The Story of Canada
Pages 86-91 – The War of 1812

A Short History of Canada
      Chapter 4 – English Canadians

The Spirit of Canada
MacDonnell on the Heights, p. 58 (War of 1812)
The Boy with an R in His Hand, p. 61
Mackenzie's Call to Rebellion, p. 63
Un Canadien Errant, p. 64

Canadian History for Dummies
Chapter 10 – The War of 1812

Concise Historical Atlas of Canada
Plate 38 – The War of 1812, 1812-1814

A History of the English Speaking Peoples – Vol. 3 The Age of Revolution
Book IX – Napoleon
      Chapter 20 – Trafalgar
      Chapter 21 – The Emperor of the French
      Chapter 22 – The Peninsular War and the Fall of Napoleon
      Chapter 23 – Washington, Adams, and Jefferson
      Chapter 24 – The War of 1812
      Chapter 25 – Elba and Waterloo

Young People's Story of Our Heritage – The Modern World
      Napoleon: The Little Giant

<u>A History of the English Speaking Peoples – Vol. 4 The Great Democracies</u>
Book X – Recovery and Reform
      Chapter 1 – The Victory Peace

<u>The Story of the World</u>
Chapter 25 – Revolution Gone Sour
      The Storming of the Bastille
      The Reign of Terror
Chapter 26 – Catherine the Great
      Princess Catherine Comes to Russia
      Catherine the Great
Chapter 27 – A Changing World
      Steam and Coal in Britain
      Cotton and Guns in America
Chapter 28 – China and the Rest of the World
      The Kingdom at the Center of the World
      The Rise of the Opium Trade

<u>The Story of the World (continued)</u>
Chapter 29 – The Rise of Bonaparte
      Napoleon Comes to Power
      The Emperor Napoleon
Chapter 30 – Freedom in the Caribbean
      The Haitian Revolt
Chapter 31 – A Different Kind of Rebellion
      The World of the Factories
      The Luddites
Chapter 32 – The Opened West
      Lewis and Clark Map the West
      Tecumseh's Resistance
Chapter 33 – The End of Napoleon
      Napoleon's Wars (And 1812, Too)
      Waterloo!
Chapter 34 – Freedom for South America
      Simon Bolivar: The Liberator
      Freedom, But Not Unity

<u>A First Book in American History</u>
Chapter 25 – William Henry Harrison
Chapter 26 – Andrew Jackson

<u>World Atlas of the Past</u>
Volume 3, pages 36-39 – Europe Under Napoleon

<u>Canada: A People's History</u>
Episode 5 – A Question of Loyalties
    Democracy and Dissent (France and England at war)
    "A Mere Matter of Marching" (Isaac Brock, Tecumseh, Thomas Jefferson)
    The Detroit Bluff (Detroit surrenders to Brock)
    Queenston Heights (John Norton, Brock is killed)
    Tecumseh's Last Stand
    "Canadians Know How to Fight!" (Canadians win at Montreal, Chrysler's Farm)
    Traitors and Heroes (Burlington Heights, Lundy's Lane)

Additional Reading

Kids' Book of Canadian History, p. 31-33
The Scout Who Led an Army (Ballantyne, L.H.)
Laura's Choice (Crook, Connie)
The Other Elizabeth (Bradford, Karleen)
Treason at York (Hayes, John Francis)
Jeremy's War 1812 (Ibbetson, John)
The Drummer Boy's Battle (Jackson, Dave & Neta)
The Soldier's Son (Leeder, Terry)
The Boy with an R in His Hand (Reaney, James)
Rebel Run (Turner, D. Harold)
A Question of Loyalty (Greenwood, Barbara)
Keep the Lights Burning, Abbie (Roop, Peter & Connie)
Revolutionary and Napoleonic Wars – History of Warfare Series (Sommerville, Donald)
Warfare in the 19th Century – History of Warfare Series (Westwell, Ian)

Part 3 – SETTLING THE NEW COUNTRY

Canadian Events/People

Colonel John By settles ByTown (later Ottawa) and builds the Rideau Canal (1826)
Joseph Montferrand (1802-1864) (Joe Mufferaw)
Catharine Parr Traill
Susanna Moodie (1832)
Joseph Brant
William Lyon Mackenzie
Louis-Joseph Papineau
Rebellion of 1837
Responsible Government (1848)

World Events/People

Jane Austin (1775-1817)
Samuel Morse invents the Electric Telegraph (1791-1872)

Core Resources

The Story of Canada
Pages 91-98 – Newcomers
Pages 98-102 – Three Native Heroes
Pages 102-105 – Rebellion and Reform
Pages 105-111 – British North America

My First History of Canada
*Note – This chapter is about moving into the west. It would fit more closely with Unit 6, "Out to the Pacific," part 2, From Canada, By Land, where David Thompson and Alexander Mackenzie are studied. I will include the material here for the sake of the continuity of this book, but feel free to skip this chapter and read it with Unit 6, or read it here where it fits more chronologically, knowing that this is a preview of what will be studied in more depth later.

Chapter 13 – The Canadians Won the Relay Race to the Pacific Ocean (1750-1810)
      Part 1 – Anthony Henday carried the baton to Alberta.
      Part 2 – Peter Pond led the Canadians into Athabaska.
      Part 3 – Alexander Mackenzie won the great relay race.
      Part 4 – Simon Fraser won the race for the Fraser River country.
      Part 5 – David Thompson lost the race for the Columbia.

A History of the English Speaking Peoples – Vol. 4 The Great Democracies
Book X – Recovery and Reform
      Chapter 2 – Canning and the Duke
      Chapter 3 – Reform and Free Trade

Additional Reading

Kids' Book of Canadian History (pg 34-37)
Backwoods of Canada (Catharine Parr Traill)
Canadian Crusoes (Catharine Parr Traill)
Roughing it in the Bush (Susanna Moodie)
Invitation to the Classics – Jane Austin (p. 203-206)
Invitation to the Classics – Johann Wolfgang von Goethe (p. 207-210)
Invitation to the Classics – William Worsdworth and Samuel Taylor Coleridge (p. 211-214)
Invitation to the Classics – John Keats (p. 221-224)
Invitation to the Classics – Alexis de Tocqueville (p. 225-228)
Invitation to the Classics – Ralph Waldo Emerson (p. 229-232)

Project Ideas

❖ Visit the Bytown Museum in Ottawa.

❖ Visit Fort Henry in Kingston, Ontario. (They actually stage a War of 1812 reenactment each year in June.)

❖ Research the history of the logging industry in Canada.

❖ Choose a Jane Austin novel to read. Remember that she wrote during some very troubled times in Europe, however she wrote in the safety of England. Does this come through in her writing? What aspect of life in the early 1800s does she emphasize?

❖ On page 105 of The Story of Canada, the Earl of Durham is quoted as saying, "I found two nations warring in the bosom of a single state." Read the paragraph explaining Durham's impression of the divided Canada, and his proposed solution for this "problem." How has his attitude affected Canada today? Has it had any impact on French/English relations? Is this attitude still present in modern day Canada? Should Durham have offered a different solution? How could Canada's fate have changed if his report to England had been different?

World Connection

❖ Listen to some works of the Beethoven. Compare and contrast his style to that of Bach, Haydn, and Mozart.

❖ How did the American Revolution affect the settlement of Canada?

❖ How did the French Revolution and the reign of Napoleon affect French/English relations? How would that affect the settlers in Canada?

❖ If you were living in Europe in 1800, what might make you consider traveling to a new land to begin a new life?

❖ Who won the War of 1812? Explain your answer. Why would the outcome of this war be in dispute? How do the perspectives of each side affect how they view the outcome? How did Britain's involvement in the Napoleonic wars in Europe affect the War of 1812 in North America?

❖ Study the famous painting of Napoleon on his horse, painted by Jacques-Louis David. What does this painting tell us about the man Napoleon?

UNIT 5 – MOVING WESTWARD

Growing up in the interior of British Columbia, there is something very personal and reminiscent for me in names like Simon Fraser and David Thompson. These names were part of the geography as I was growing up, so it is very interesting to read about the men these rivers were named for, and to discover how they fit into the history of our country. I found particularly interesting the story Donalda Dickie tells of John Tod and Lolo, Chief of the Shuswaps in chapter 14 of <u>My First History of Canada</u>. Since I spent most of my youth in Kamloops, having skied on Tod Mountain, and driven up Mt. Lolo, it is fascinating to learn whom those landmarks were named for, and to learn some history of the area that we were not taught in school. I hope you are also finding personal connections to your studies as we learn about the people who discovered, settled, and ruled your neighbourhood long ago.

Part 1 – FUR TRADERS

Canadian Events/People

Samuel Hearne (1745-1792)
Pontiac (1769)
Alexander Mackenzie (1763-1820)
Simon Fraser
David Thompson

World Events/People

Industrial Revolution (1700s/1800s)

Core Resources

<u>The Story of Canada</u>
Chapter 5, pages 114-118 – The Great Northwest
Pages 118-122 – The Fur Traders' Rivalry

<u>The Spirit of Canada</u>
A Coppermine Feast (Samuel Hearne) p. 37
The Long Journey of "Our Dog" (Mackenzie) p. 39
Northwest Passage (Franklin & Kelsey) p. 44

<u>Concise Historical Atlas of Canada</u>
Plate 44 – France Secures the Interior, 1740-1755
Plate 45 – The Migratory Fisheries, 18th Century
Plate 46 – The Newfoundland Fishery, 18th Century

<u>The Story of the World</u>
Chapter 35 – Mexican Independence
      The Cry of Dolores
      The Republic of Mexico

<u>Canada: A People's History</u>
Episode 6 – The Pathfinders (1670-1850)
      Life at the Bay (David Thompson a Hudson's Bay clerk)
      A Journey to the North (Samuel Hearne)
      The Nor'Westers
      In the Shadow of the Rockies (David Thompson)
      The Voyageurs (Daniel Harmon)
      The Winterer (Daniel Harmon)
      Looking at Stars (David Thompson learns surveying and charts the northwest)

Additional Reading

The Savage River: Seventy-One Days with Simon Fraser (Campbell, Marjorie Wilkins)
A Dog Came, Too (Manson, Ainslie)
On Foot to the Arctic (Symes, R.)
Alexander Mackenzie (Manson, Ainslie)
Pontiac: Mighty Ottawa Chief (Voight, V.)
The Map-Maker (David Thompson) (Wood, Kerry)
From Sea to Sea: Alexander Mackenzie
Footprints in the Snow, p. 26 (Alexander Mackenzie)
Footprints in the Snow, p. 30 (David Thompson)
The Last 500 Years (Usborne), p. 46-55

Part 2 – THE METIS

Canadian Events/People

First Western Settlement - Red River

World Events/People

Hans Christian Anderson (1805-1875)
Richard Wagner (1813-1883)
Charles Darwin (1809-1882)
Florence Nightingale
Crimean War (1853-1856)

Core Resources

The Story of Canada
Pages 122-125 – The People in Between
Pages 125-126 – The Red River War

My First History of Canada
Chapter 14 – Red River Was the First Settlement in Western Canada (1811-1866)
        Part 1 – The Silver Chief started the Red River settlement.
        Part 2 – The Nor'Westers tried to destroy Red River.
        Part 3 – The two companies united as the Hudson's Bay Company.
        Part 4 – Governor George Simpson was young and merry.
        Part 5 – Enter British Columbia

A Short History of Canada
        Chapter 7 – The Great Northwest

Canada: A People's History
Episode 6 – The Pathfinders
        The Selkirk Settlers (Nor'Westers against the Hudson's Bay Men)
        Seven Oaks (Nor'Westers merge with Hudson's Bay Co.)

A History of the English Speaking Peoples – Vol. 4 The Great Democracies
Book X – Recovery and Reform
        Chapter 4 – The Crimean War
        Chapter 5 – Palmerston

Young People's Story of Our Heritage – The Modern World
        Europe Moves Toward National Unity
        Other Nations Develop
        Industrial Revolution

<u>The Story of the World – Volume 4</u>
Chapter 1 -   Britains Empire
                     Victoria's England
                     The Sepoy Mutiny
Chapter 2 -   West Against East
                     Japan Re-Opens
                     The Crimean War
Chapter 3 -   British Invasions
                     The Great Game
                     Wandering Through Africa
Chapter 4 -   Resurrection and Rebellion
                     Italy's "Resurrection"
                     The Taiping Rebellion

Additional Reading

Riel's People: How the Metis Lived (How They Lived in Canada series)
Ian of Red River (Guttormsson, Ragnhildur)
The Trouble with Jamie (McLaughlin, Lorie)
Red River Adventure (Chalmers, J.W.)
Hans Christian Anderson (Greene, Carol)
Any collection of Hans Christian Anderson stories
Invitation to the Classics – Frederick Douglass (p. 233-236)
Invitation to the Classics – Nathaniel Hawthorne (p. 237-240)

Part 3 – THE PIONEERS

Canadian Events/People

Pioneers settle the plains

World Events/People

Louis Braille (1809-1852)
Dr. Marcus & Narcissa Whitman (1843)
Elizabeth Blackwell (1821-1910)

Core Resources

The Story of Canada
Pages 126-128 – The Bay's Empire
Pages 129-132 – Wanderers and Artists
Pages 132-135 – Leaders of the West

My First History of Canada
Chapter 15 – The Pioneers (1815-1850)
       Part 1 – Next came the pioneers: they worked hard.
       Part 2 – The pioneers had fun too.
       Part 3 – The pioneers were great builders.
       Part 4 – Canada got two new kinds of business.

A History of the English Speaking Peoples – Vol. 4 The Great Democracies
Book X – Recovery and Reform
       Chapter 6 – The Migration of the Peoples I
       Chapter 7 – The Migration of the Peoples II

Concise Historical Atlas of Canada
Plate 19 – The Emergence of a Transportation System, 1837-1852

Canada: A People's History
Episode 6 – The Pathfinders
       The Little Emperor (George Simpson)

Additional Reading

A Pioneer Story (Greenwood, Barbara)
Pioneer Crafts (Greenwood, Barbara)
Ghost Town at Sundown (Magic Treehouse Series) (Osborne, Mary)
A Picture Book of Louise Braille (Adler, David)
Louis Braille (Kugelmass, J. Alvin)
Attack in the Rye Grass (Jackson, Dave & Neta)
The Doll (Taylor, Cora)
Ida and the Wool Smugglers (Alderson, Sue Ann)
Pioneer Girl (Caswell, Maryanne)
Sarah Plain and Tall (MacLachlan, Patricia)
Skylark (MacLachlan, Patricia)
Carolina's Courage (Unwin, Nora)
Storm Child (Bellingham, Brenda)
Elizabeth Blackwell: First Woman Doctor (Green, Carol)
Eliza's Best Wednesday (Lalonde, C.)
Pirates Past Noon (Magic Treehouse Series) (Osborne, Mary)
Little House on the Prairie series (Wilder, Laura Ingalls)

Part 4 – THE PRAIRIES

Canadian Events/People

North West Mounted Police
Sitting Bull

World Events/People

Alexander Graham Bell (1847-1922)
Charles Dickens (1812-1870)
Emily Dickinson (1830-1886)

Core Resources

My First History of Canada
Chapter 16 – Bringing in the Prairies (1850-1885)
        Part 1 – The people of the great plains.
            The Indians hunt the buffalo
            The bad men
        Part 2 – Canada sent the North West Mounted Police to keep order.
            Prairie Chicken Old Man
            The Sitting Bull Story
        Part 3 – The Canadians built the Canadian Pacific Railway to tie the provinces together.

The Spirit of Canada
A Letter from Shinguacouse, p. 107
The Ballad of Crowfoot, p. 109
Canadian Indian Place Names, p. 267

Additional Reading

Boldly Canadian: The story of the RCMP (Hamilton-Barry, Joann)
Forts of Canada
People of the Buffalo (How They Lived in Canada series)
Song of the Pines (Havighurst, Walter & Marion)
Bugles in the Hills (Hayes, John Francis)
The Queen's Cowboy (Colonel MacLeod) (Wood, Kerry)
Emily Dickinson (Greene, Carol)
Any work by Dickens
Invitation to the Classics – Emily Dickinson (p. 241-244)
Invitation to the Classics – Herman Melville (p. 245-248)
Invitation to the Classics – Gustave Flaubert (p. 249-252)
Invitation to the Classics – Charles Dickens (p. 259-262)
Invitation to the Classics – John Henry, Cardinal Newman (p. 263-266)

Project Ideas

- ❖ Visit the RCMP Museum in Regina, Saskatchewan.

- ❖ Research the beginnings of the Northwest Mounted Police (later named the Royal Canadian Mounted Police). Some RCMP related web sites can be found at **www.rcmpmuseum.com/sites.htm**

- ❖ Visit any of the sites named for people you have studied. (eg. the Fraser River, the Thompson River, Mount Lolo, Tod Mountain)

- ❖ Visit Head-Smashed-In Buffalo Jump in southern Alberta, or visit their web site, **www.head-smashed-in.com,** and find out about the buffalo (Do you know how fast a buffalo can run while stampeding?) and the history of the Blackfoot people. There are special events every Sunday, so check the web site if you're going to be in the area. They even offer a campout in a tipi!

- ❖ Compare/contrast the way the Canadians dealt with the Native People with the way the Americans dealt with them. Comment on the pros and cons of both methods/attitudes.

- ❖ Research the origin of the name of your town or a local river, lake, mountain or other landmark. Many have Native Indian names, and many were named for the Europeans who first discovered or settled an area. But there are many other interesting origins for the names of places. Here is a website to get you started: **http://geonames.nrcan.gc.ca/education/index_e.php**

World Connection

- ❖ Life in 1850 was much different from life just 100 years before. Many changes began to take place in Europe through the 1700s and 1800s. The Industrial Revolution was all about industry, yet it affected the lives of virtually all people. How did the Renaissance thinking in the 1600s help lead the way to the Industrial Revolution? How had the Revolution affected life in Europe by the mid 1800s? Can you find examples in some of the literature you have read for this study? How did these effects carry over into the New World? How did the desire for world exploration affect the changes of the Industrial Revolution? How did the Industrial Revolution change navigation?

- ❖ Research the invention of a machine from the late 1700s or early 1800s. How did that machine affect the lives of the people?

- ❖ Create an invention of your own!

❖ Listen to some of the works of Richard Wagner. How does his music differ from those you studied in previous lessons? (Bach, Beethoven, etc.)

❖ Charles Dickens gave us a good picture of life in England in the 1800s in his books. Compare/contrast this with life in Canada at the same time.

❖ Read Darwin's <u>Origin of the Species</u>, followed by <u>Darwin's Black Box</u>, by Michael Behe. How have Darwin's ideas affected how we view the world? Why do you think his ideas have survived for so long? Do you think Renaissance thinking had a part in the development of Darwin's ideas?

UNIT 6 – OUT TO THE PACIFIC

Although I haven't lived in BC for over 15 years, or maybe because of that, I found this unit particularly fun to put together! I apologize if I seem to be favouring the westernmost Province in this study, but that is the beauty of putting your own study together - you can delve in great, passionate depths into the area that is closest to your heart!

"Meanwhile back at the ranch...." is the phrase that comes to mind when I read Chapter 6 in The Story of Canada. We have read about the history of Canada up to about 1860, but are now stepping back in time to focus for a moment on the West. We will back up nearly 100 years to the time of the Nootka and their Chief, Maquinna; to the time when the first white men mingled and traded with the native people on the west coast. We will see men from the east finally finishing their long, eager search for the Pacific. We will watch this newest colony's growth explode with the greed of the Gold Rush.

Since we have already covered this period, I have not included much in the way of world events. However, there were a few things happening in the United States that are somewhat related to the development of the colony of British Columbia. First, the California Gold Rush led to the search for the "mother lode," pushing prospectors further and further north. This search played a major role in the growth of British Columbia when gold was discovered in the Fraser River. Next, the Mexican/American war shows how the United States developed its west during this same time period. I think it is an interesting study to compare this with how western Canada began and grew.

This unit lends itself to a division of three parts. As always, spend as much time per section as you need. If you are planning one month per unit, simply spill one or two of these sections over into another week. Or, since we already studied the west coast Indians in the first unit, do a more cursory review of them now and divide the month in half for the other two parts of this unit.

Part 1 – THE WEST COAST

Canadian Events/People

Nootka Indians
James Cook (1778)
John Meares (1789)
Chief Maquinna
George Vancouver (1792)

World Events/People

This unit goes back to early life in and discovery of North America, as it pertains specifically to the west coast. Therefore, there are no corresponding world events to study that have not already been covered.

Core Resources

The Story of Canada
Pages 138-139 – Mountains and Oceans
Pages 140-141 – The Nootka Traders
Pages 142-146 – People of the Salmon

The Story of the World
Chapter 36 – The Slave Trade Ends
        The Work of the Abolitionists
Chapter 37 – Troubled Africa
        The Zulu Kingdom
        The Boers and the British

Canada: A People's History
Episode 1 – When the World Began
        Pacific (James Cook)
        An Air of Savage Magnificence (Nootka Indians)
        Captivity (John Jewitt)

Additional Reading

Sea and Cedar: How the Northwest Coast Indians Lived (How They Lived in Canada Series) (McConkey, Lois)
Anything you used for the first unit, pertaining specifically to the West Coast Indians

Part 2 – FROM CANADA, BY LAND

Canadian Events/People

Alexander MacKenzie (1763-1820)
Simon Fraser
David Thompson

World Events/People

Opium War (China)
The Alamo and the Mexican/American War

Core Resources

The Story of Canada
Pages 146-151 – From Canada, By Land
Pages 151-155 – The Father of British Columbia

A History of the English Speaking Peoples – Vol. 4 The Great Democracies
Book XI – The Great Republic
      Chapter 8 – American Epic

Concise Historical Atlas of Canada
Plate 8 – Exploration in the Far Northwest, 18th and 19th Centuries

The Story of the World
Chapter 38 – American Tragedies
      The Trail of Tears
      Nat Turner's Revolt
Chapter 39 – China Adrift
      The First Opium War
Chapter 40 – Mexico and Her Neighbor
      Remember the Alamo
      The Mexican-American War

Canada: A People's History
Episode 6 – The Pathfinders
      From Canada by Land (Alexander Mackenzie, David Thompson)
      The Columbia (David Thompson reaches the Pacific)
      The Masterwork (David Thompson's map)
      A New Era (Fur trade dwindles, David Thompson's last years)

Additional Reading

(These resources were mentioned in the last unit, but could be used in either Unit 5 or 6.)

The Map-Maker (David Thompson) (Wood, Kerry)
From Sea to Sea: Alexander MacKenzie
Footprints in the Snow, p. 26 (Alexander MacKenzie)
Footprints in the Snow, p. 30 (David Thompson)
The Last 500 Years (Usborne), p. 60-65 (new this unit)

Part 3 – THE FRASER RIVER GOLD RUSH

Canadian Events/People

James Douglas (1843)
Fraser River Gold Rush (1858)
Billy Barker
Cariboo Cameron
Robert Dunsmuir
"Gassy" Jack Deighton (Founder of Gastown, which became Vancouver)

World Events/People

California Gold Rush (1849)

Core Resources

The Story of Canada
Pages 155-157 – The Gold Fields
Pages 158-159 – Mountains and Oceans

The Spirit of Canada
The stories I have chosen may not fit the time period exactly, but they match the subject matter of this Unit, so I thought this a good time to read them. The Klondike Gold Rush will be studied briefly in Unit 8, so "Sam McGee" and "Ice Worms" could be saved until then. One word of caution: You may want to pre-read "The Cremation of Sam McGee" before reading it with younger children!

The Log Jam, p. 89
Way Up the Ucletaw, p. 94
Ti-Jean Brings Home the Moon, p. 159
Paul Bunyan Digs the St. Lawrence River, p. 162
The Cremation of Sam McGee, p. 98 (Klondike Gold Rush)
When the Ice Worms Nest Again, p. 239

The Story of the World
Chapter 41 – New Zealand and Her Rulers
          The Treaty of Waitangi
          The New Zealand Wars
Chapter 42 – The World of Forty-Nine
          The Gold Rush
          A World of Unrest

Canada: A People's History
Episode 6 – The Pathfinders
          The Gold Rush (James Douglas, Billy Barker, Samuel Hathaway)

Additional Reading

Kids' Book of Canadian History, pg. 38-41 (The Underground Railroad is mentioned in this selection, and will be studied in the next Unit.)
The Gold Miner's Rescue (Jackson, Dave & Neta)
Invitation to the Classics – Soren Kierkegaard (p. 267-270)

Project Ideas

❖ If you live in the west and have been longing to visit some of the sites you've been studying about, your chance is finally here! I found a couple of websites of British Columbia historical attractions at **www.britishcolumbia.com/attractions** (scroll down for historical sites) and **www.airhighways.com/bc.htm** Some suggestions for field trips based on this unit follow. If you can't make it to these places, check out the web sites for lots of great information. It's almost like being there!

- Any West Coast Indian Village ('Ksan Village at Hazleton, BC is one I remember visiting as a child. The website is **www.ksan.org**)
- Barkerville, BC **www.barkerville.ca**
- Gastown, Vancouver **www.seegastown.com**
- Dunsmuir's Craigdarroch Castle, Victoria **www.craigdarrochcastle.com/**
- Ft. Rodd Hill/Fisguard Lighthouse, Esquimalt **www.britishcolumbia.com/attractions/?id=65**
- Tour a sawmill
- Tour a fish cannery

❖ Choose one of the colourful characters in this unit and research more about him/her. Write an essay, a play (or video), or a poem about this person's life, or come up with your own creative project! (A neat idea can be found in Footprints in the Snow, p. 43-50.)

❖ The West Coast Indians have a very distinctive style of art. Create your own original design based on this style. There are some black & white examples in the book Sea and Cedar. For full colour examples, see **www.totemcarver.com/index_js.html** For written directions and the history of this artwork, see **www.mala.bc.ca/www/discover/educate/posters/jodid.htm**

❖ Build a West Coast Indian village. Use popsicle sticks for logs for the long houses. Sticks could be totem poles. If you really want to get creative, try carving tiny canoes and paint stick totem poles! (Or get dowels and carve/paint them.)

❖ Map the routes taken by George Vancouver and Alexander MacKenzie. Write a conversation that could have taken place between them if the two had met in Bella Coola.

❖ Write a story based on the following: Imagine you live in a remote place that few people know of and/or it is difficult to get to. (This could be on Earth or in space!) Something "valuable" is found. (It could be something rare, precious, or crazy!) Tell the story of the people who "risk it all" to reach your land and find the treasure. Remember to describe how life changes for those living in this faraway place when the adventurers begin to arrive.

❖ Try panning for gold! I found instructions at **www.goldgold.com/panninginstructions.htm** At the bottom of the page is how to use lead instead of gold. To make it more fun, paint the lead pieces gold. Another approach can be found at **www.tustin.k12.ca.us/cyberseminar/gold.htm** It is specifically geared for primary level classrooms, and deals with the California Gold Rush. But this web page has lots of great ideas that could easily be incorporated into a "Gold Rush Day" for your homeschool group, or just your own children.

World Connection

❖ The famous "Alamo" battle occurred in 1836. This is one of those events everyone has heard about, but as Canadians we aren't taught what it was all about in school. What does "Remember the Alamo" mean? **www.americanwest.com/pages/alamo.htm** is a website to help get your research going. Also, several movies have been made about this event. Once you've discovered all about the Alamo and the Mexican/American war that followed, compare and contrast how the Western United States was formed with the development of British Columbia.

❖ The California Gold Rush preceded the Fraser River Gold Rush, which preceded the Klondike Gold Rush. How did each lead into the next? With all the Americans moving north to find gold in the Fraser River, James Douglas was afraid the US might try to annex the area we know as British Columbia. How might the formation of British Columbia been different if most of the increase in population had come from Canada?

UNIT 7 – CONFEDERATION

Unit 7 covers an exciting time in Canada's history: The days of Confederation! There was a lot going on in the world during this time, and a lot going on in Canada. You could easily spend more than a month on this unit if you want to study it in more detail.

While Canada was becoming a brand new nation, her neighbour to the south, nearly a century old already, was at war with herself. Canada played an important role in the freeing of slaves during that time, and I think it deserves a deeper look than that given in The Story of Canada. Therefore, I have devoted one part of this unit to the Underground Railroad. This is a time when Canada shone as a hero. Canada was far from perfect, but she offered freedom to those willing to make the long trek to the north to find her safe haven. The CBC has broadcast a special on this topic, called "Freedom's Land: Canada and the Underground Railroad." It was part of a series called, "The Canadian Experience."

(**www.cbc.ca/canadianexperience/freedomsland**) It did not treat Canada in as positive a light as I would have liked, but it was very informative and worth watching with older students if you can find a copy. (Due to the beatings and other sensitive subject matter shown plainly in the video, I would not recommend it for younger students.)

This is also an ideal time to begin a study of Canadian Government. As you study the BNA Act and read about the difficulties of joining such a vast area into one nation, trace the beginnings of our parliamentary system. In future units watch how the democratic process is adapted as the country changes and grows, new parties are begun, and old ones die, until you reach, at the end of the study, the political landscape we see before us today. Look at how world events and domestic difficulties and prosperities affected the way the government looked and the way it functioned. A whole study could be made of this one aspect of Canadian History. For most of us, however, it will be enough to follow it as a sideline to our study of the major events in Canada's history. Some resources for this project are listed in the projects section for this unit. There is also a more detailed list of resources for studying Canadian Government at the end of this guide.

Part 1 - CONFEDERATION

Canadian Events/People

John A. McDonald
George Brown
D'Arcy McGee
Charles Tupper, Premier of NS
George Coles
Joseph Howe

World Events/People

Queen Victoria
David Livingston
Tolstoy (War and Peace, 1864)
Lewis Caroll (Alice in Wonderland, 1865)
The International Red Cross is founded in Switzerland (1865)
Dostoyevsky (Crime & Punishment, 1866)
US buys Alaska from Russia (1867)
Louisa M. Alcott (Little Women, 1868)
Renoir
Strauss
Verdi
Jules Verne (20,000 Leagues Under the Sea, 1869)

Core Resources

The Story of Canada
Chapter 7, pages 162-165 – Confederation Days
Pages 165-166 – Breaking the Deadlock
Pages 166-169 – The Idea of Confederation
Pages 170-171 – From Charlottetown to Quebec
Pages 172-178 – The Battle for Confederation

My First History of Canada
Chapter 17 – The Provinces United to Make Our Canada (1850-1885)
    Part 1 – The provinces were growing up.
    Part 2 – The provinces all built schools and colleges.
    Part 3 – The Assemblies made the Governors and Councils do what the
        people wanted.
    Part 4 – Four of the provinces united to form the Dominion of Canada.

Canada: A People's History
Episode 8 – The Great Enterprise (1850-1867)
    (John A. McDonald, American Civil War)
    "I Am a French Canadian" (George Etienne Cartier)
    "A Sly Fox" (John A. McDonald)
    "We Have Two Countries" (George Brown, "Rep by Pop")
    The People of British North America
    Hope Gate (Irish Immigrants, D'Arcy McGee)
    "City of Wealth"
    A Winter of Utter Misery
    "To Have the Power" (George Brown)
    Strangers in Charlottetown (Charlottetown Conference)
    Three Weeks in Quebec
    "Let Their Memory Be Dark" (Opposition in Quebec)
    "Good Management and Means" (Charles Tupper, Joseph Howe, Fenian Uprising)
    "A Great Revolution" (Delegates to London, BNA Act passed)
    July 1, 1867

Additional Reading

Kids' Book of Canadian History, p. 38-44
Kids' Book of Canadian Prime Ministers, p. 8-14
Footprints in the Snow, p. 60 (Sir John A. MacDonald)
Footprints in the Snow, p. 58 (Dr. James Barry)
Footprints in the Snow, p. 63 (The St. John 4)
Footprints in the Snow, p. 66 (D'Arcy McGee)
Footprints in the Snow, p. 69 (Joseph Howe)
Footprints in the Snow, p. 71 (Amor de Cosmos)
A Truly Loyal Subject: George Brown and Confederation (Marquis, Vince)
The Last 500 Years, p. 56-57 (The Scramble for Africa)
Louisa May Alcott: Author, Nurse, Suffragate (Greene, Carol)
Government: Participating in Canada (Quinlan, Don)
Invitation to the Classics – George Eliot (p. 271-274)
Invitation to the Classics – Gerard Manley Hopkins (p. 275-278)
Invitation to the Classics – Leo Tolstoy (p. 279-282)
The Book of Rule: How the World is Governed (Dorling Kindersley Limited)

Part 2 – UNDERGROUND RAILROAD

Canadian Events/People

Underground Railroad to Canada

World Events/People

U.S. Civil War (1861-1865)
Abraham Lincoln (1809-1865)
Mark Twain (The Adventures of Tom Sawyer, 1876)

Core Resources

The Story of Canada
Page 164 – Follow the Drinking Gourd

The Spirit of Canada
Follow the Drinking Gourd, p. 67
The Underground Railroad, p. 69
A Visit from the Slave Catcher, p. 71

A History of the English Speaking Peoples – Vol. 4 The Great Democracies
Book XI – The Great Republic
      Chapter 9 – Slavery and Secession
      Chapter 10 – The Union in Danger
      Chapter 11 – The Campaign Against Richmond
      Chapter 12 – Lee and McClellan
      Chapter 13 – Chancellorsville and Gettysburg
      Chapter 14 – The Victory of the Union

The Story of the World – Volume 4
Chapter 5 -   The American Civil War
           South Against North
           After the Civil War

A First Book in American History
Chapter 29 – Early Life of Abraham Lincoln
Chapter 30 – Lincoln in Public Life
Chapter 31 – Something About the Great Civil War

Canada: A People's History
Episode 8 – The Great Enterprise
       The Underground Railroad

Additional Reading

The Last 500 Years, p. 58-61 (The American Civil War)
Brady (Fritz, Jean)
The Last Safe House (Greenwood, Barbara)
Listen for the Whippoorwill (Jackson, Dave & Neta)
Go Free or Die: Harriet Tubman (Lerner Biography available from Tree of Life)
If You Traveled on the Underground Railroad (Levine, Ellen)
Underground to Canada (Smucker, Barbara)
The Adventures of Tom Sawyer (Twain, Mark)
The Adventures of Huckleberry Finn (Twain, Mark)
Abraham Lincoln (D'Aulaire)
Invitation to the Classics – Mark Twain (p. 291-294)
The American Civil War – History of Warfare Series
Uncle Tom's Cabin (Harriet Beecher Stowe)

Part 3 – RIEL REBELLION

Canadian Events/People

Red River Uprising (1869)
William McDougall
Louis Riel
Thomas Scott
PEI Joins Canada (1873)
James Pope
Cypress Hills Massacre (1873)
Indian Act (1876)
Crowfoot's Treaty (1877)

World Events/People

Franco-Prussian War (1870-1871)
Brahms
Monet
Bizet
Alexander Graham Bell invents the telephone (1876)
Russo-Turkish War (1876-1878)
Thomas Edison invents the phonograph (1877)
William Booth and the Salvation Army (1878)

Core Resources

The Story of Canada
Pages 178-185 – Into the West

My First History of Canada
Chapter 17, Part 5 – Red River made her choice.
      Part 6 – The Metis rebellion.
      Part 7 – Gold! Gold on the Fraser! (We studied in the gold rush in the last
          unit. This section could be read then or saved to read in order as a
          review now.)

The Spirit of Canada
The Ballad of Crowfoot, p. 109
Address to the Jury, p. 119
Song of Louis Riel, p. 120

Additional Reading

Kids' Book of Canadian History, p. 45-46
Kids' Book of Canadian Prime Ministers, p. 10-11
Buckskin Brigadier (McCourt, Edward)
The Bold Heart (Phelan, Josephine)
Reil's People ("How They Lived in Canada" Series)

Part 4 – CANADIAN PACIFIC RAILROAD

Canadian Events/People

Railway Finished Nov. 7, 1885
Louis Riel hanged Nov. 1885

World Events/People

Louis Pasteur
War of the Pacific (Chili, Bolivia,
Peru) (1881-1884)
Tchaikovsky (1812 Overture
1882)
Robert Louis Stevenson
(Treasure Island, 1882)
Nietzsche
Karl Marx (Das Kapital vol. 2,
1885)
Van Gogh

Core Resources

The Story of Canada
Pages 185-186 – The Whole
Nation Minus One
Pages 187-193 – The Great Railway

My First History of Canada
Chapter 18 – The Eastern Provinces Went Into New Industries (1850-1895)
    Part 1 – Nova Scotia went into coal and steel.
    Part 2 – Quebec led the way in mining.
    Part 3 – New Brunswick made new uses of her timber.
    Part 4 – Prince Edward Island invented fox farming.
    Part 5 – Newfoundland found an iron mine and built a railway.
    Part 6 – Ontario had the first oil wells in Canada.

Flashback Canada
Chapter 20 – The Steel Riboon
Chapter 21 – An Almost Impossible Task
Chapter 22 – The Last Spike
Chapter 23 – The Sod House Frontier
Chapter 24 – The Rebellion of 1885
Chapter 25 – The Rebels on Trial
Chapter 26 – The Father of Canada Dies

A Short History of Canada
Part II – A Mari Usque ad Mare
      Chapter 3 – National Policy
      Chapter 4 – Political Revolution

Discovering Canada: The Railways (Livesey, Robert)

The Spirit of Canada
Canadian Railroad Trilogy, p. 123
Spirits of the Railway, p. 126
The Lady and the Cowcatcher, p. 130

A History of the English Speaking Peoples – Vol. 4 The Great Democracies
Book XII – The Victorian Age
      Chapter 16 – Gladstone and Disraeli
      Chapter 17 – American "Reconstruction"

The Story of the World – Volume 4
Chapter 6 - Two Tries for Freedom
            Paraguay and the Triple Alliance
            The Dominion of Canada
Chapter 7 - Two Empires, Three Republics, and One Kingdom
            Two Empires and Three Republics
            The Second Reich
Chapter 8 - Becoming Modern
            Rails, Zones, and Bulbs
            Japan's Meiji Restoration
Chapter 9 - Two More Empires, Two Rebellions
            The Dutch East Indies
            The Sick Man of Europe
Chapter 10 - A Canal to the East and a Very Dry Desert
            The War of the Pacific
            The Suez Canal
Chapter 11 - The Far Parts of the World
            The Iron Outlaw
            Carving Up Africa

Concise Historical Atlas of Canada
Plate 20 – Linking Canada, 1867-1891

Canada: A People's History
Episode 9 – From Sea to Sea
      "Tie the Oceans Together (Amour de Cosmos, Railway promised to BC)
      "For the Good of the Dominion" (CPR Scandal, Cartier dies)

Additional Reading

Kids' Book of Canadian History, p. 47-50
Kids' Book of Canada's Railway
Louis Pasteur: Enemy of Disease (Greene, Carol)
A Child's Garden of Verses (Stevenson, Robert Louis)
Invitation to the Classics – Fyodor Dostoyevsky (p. 283-286)
Invitation to the Classics – Henry James (p. 287-290)
Invitation to the Classics – Friedrich Nietzsche (p. 299-302)

Project Ideas

❖ Research the history of Canadian Government and/or how our
   government works today. Some resources to get you started:

   - Government: Participating in Canada, by Don Quinlan
   - Canada Votes: How We Elect Our Government, by Linda Granfield
   - A CD-ROM, which can be received free from the Government by
     requesting it at this site **www.tinyurl.com/2149b**, is an excellent
     introduction to the electoral system. It is set up in the form of a
     map, and children can go to any building on the map to get
     information about that part of the system. Once they have
     discovered all they can, a quiz game can be played alone or with a
     second player. Lots of fun, and lots of information! This is a great
     vehicle for introducing the subject to middle school students.

❖ Older children, particularly those interested in the political history of
   Canada, might appreciate reading the actual BNA Act. It can be found on-
   line at **www.solon.org/Constitutions/Canada/English/ca_1867.html**
   Many other interesting historical documents (such as the Charter of
   Hudson's Bay, the Quebec Act of 1774, and many others) can be found at
   www.solon.org/Constitutions/Canada/English/index.html

❖ Draw a map of the eastern US and Canada (or find an outline map online),
   and draw in the routes taken by the slaves on the underground railroad to
   Canada.

❖ As the provinces join confederation in your studies, do some research on
   the geography and culture of each province. Some books to start with:

   - The Big Book of Canada, by Christopher Moore (Lots of neat facts
     about all facets of life in each province, including recipes and local
     songs and stories.)
   - Kids' Book of Canada, by Barbara Greenwood

❖ The completion of the cross-Canada railway was of major importance to the formation of the country. Research the invention of the steam engine and the history of rail travel around the world. Alternatively, write a paper explaining why the railway was so important to the formation of Canada.

❖ If you are in the west, visit the site of the last spike at Craigellachi, British Columbia (south-west of Revelstoke on Hwy 1) (**www.revelstokecc.bc.ca/vacation/lspike.htm**)

❖ If you are in Alberta or Saskatchewan, visit Fort Battleford where you will see where the North West Mounted Police lived, and hear the story of Louis Riel. The official website is **www.pc.gc.ca/lhn-nhs/sk/battleford/index_E.asp**. This Saskatchewan website also had good information on the history of the site: **www.virtualsk.com/current_issue/fort_battleford.html**.

❖ Fort Garry in Manitoba is another great site to visit. Learn more about it at **www.pc.gc.ca/lhn-nhs/mb/fortgarry/index_e.asp**

World Connection

❖ Do a more in-depth study of the American Civil War, including the beginning of slavery in North America, what perpetuated it, and how it ended. Read Uncle Tom's Cabin, by Harriet Beecher Stowe, Up from Slavery, by Booker T. Washington, and other books on the subject. Write an essay on the ethics of slavery.

❖ Listen to the works of the composers of this time period. How does their music differ from that of the earlier composers? How did the changes in thought through exploration, invention, and other modern ideas affect the changes in music during this time? Some books on music history that might help you in understanding the development of music:

- The Gift of Music, by Jane Stuart and Betty Carlson
- Lives of the Musicians (Good Times, Bad Times and What the Neighbours Thought), by Kathleen Krull
- Books from the "Masters of Music" series
- The Enjoyment of Music, by Joseph Machlis

❖ Art has also been changing throughout history. Compare the changes in art during the Victorian era with the changes in music at the same time. For a historical look at art, try The Annotated Mona Lisa, by Carol Strickland, or other books on art history.

❖ Literature, like art and music, has evolved over time, affected by world events and popular thought. Compare its evolution with that of music and/or art. Look for any anthology of literature to help with this. My favourite book, because of its accessibility to those of us who are not well educated in literature, is <u>Invitation to the Classics</u>, by Louise Cowan and Os Guinness.

❖ The time Queen Victoria reigned in England (1837-1901) is known as the Victorian Era. Compare life in Victorian England with life in Canada during this time.

❖ Research the life of any of the people associated with this time period

UNIT 8 – LAURIER'S SUNNY WAYS

This unit does not divide neatly into four parts as most of the others have done; therefore, the sections outlined below are very subjective. Organize this unit in whatever way works best for you. What I have done is to separate out some of the political aspects of the era, and combined it with the Klondike Gold Rush for part 1. If you did not research the Gold Rush in Unit 6, this would be a good time to go back and check out my ideas and apply them to the Klondike Gold Rush.

For part 2 I have listed readings that specifically talk about life around the turn of the century. This is what most of the reading in our main texts is about for this unit, and as you can see, there is a plethora of additional material available! Spend more time on this part of the unit if you are interested.

Part 3 returns to the political scene of the time, looking specifically at Canada's role in the world as she begins to look at world involvement, taking part in a foreign conflict for the first time.

This whole unit seems to denote a transitional time. A time between Canada's beginnings - domestic wars and land disputes, bringing in the west and defining Canada's borders - and the Canada we know today - a country in her own right, involved in the world as she chooses to be. Advances in technology were changing our way of life. Canada was beginning to look beyond herself to define her place in the world. As you read, consider how the events of this time began to mold the country into the Canada of the 21st Century, how similar our views as a nation are today, and how our views and ways of life have changed since the beginning of the 20th century.

Part 1 – LAURIER AND THE GOLD RUSH

Canadian Events/People

Laurier Prime Minister (1896-1911)
Klondike Gold Rush

World Events/People

Freud, (1856-1939)
Sino-French War, (1883-1885)
Spanish-American War (1898)

Core Resources

The Story of Canada
Chapter 8, pages 196-197 – Sunny Ways
Pages 198-200 – Gold Fever

Concise Historical Atlas of Canada
Plate 10 – From Sea to Sea: Territorial Growth to 1900
Plate 14 – The Canadian Population, 1871, 1891
Plate 15 – The Exodus: Migrations, 1860-1900
Plate 25 – Canada in 1891
Plate 30 – The Look of Domestic Building, 1891
Plate 31 – The Printed Word, 18th and 19th Centuries
Plate 32 – The Quest for Universal Schooling, 1851-1891
Plate 56 – The Developing Industrial Heartland, 1871-1891
Plate 57 – Social Change in Montreal, 1842-1901
Plate 64 – Gold and Population in British Columbia, 1858-1881

A First Book in American History
Chapter 32 – Something About the Spanish War
Chapter 33 – Great Expositions
Chapter 34 – The Panama Canal
Chapter 35 – How the United States Became Larger (An Object Lesson in Historic Geography)

Canada: A People's History
Episode 11 – The Great Transformation (1896-1915)
        (Klondike Gold Rush)
        "The Sunny Way" (Wilfrid Laurier, Manitoba Schools Question)
        "Not a Practical Mind" (Boer War, Henri Bourassa)

Additional Reading

Kids' Book of Canadian History, p. 51-52 "A New Era"
Kids' Book of Canadian Prime Ministers, p. 15 (Abbott)
Kids' Book of Canadian Prime Ministers, p.16 (Thompson)
Kids' Book of Canadian Prime Ministers, p.17 (Boswell)
Kids' Book of Canadian Prime Ministers, p.18 (Tupper)
Kids' Book of Canadian Prime Ministers, p.19-22 (Laurier) The Golden Trail (Berton, Pierre)
Footprints in the Snow, p. 94 (Sam Steele)
Footprints in the Snow, p. 107 (Wilfred Grenfell)
Footprints in the Snow, p. 129 (Joe Boyle)
Invitation to the Classics – Joseph Conrad (p. 303-306)
Editorial and Political Cartooning (Hoff, Syd)

Part 2 – THE LAST BEST WEST

Canadian Events/People

Homesteading on the Prairies
Immigrants come to Canada
Alberta & Saskatchewan become Provinces, 1905
Marquis Wheat
Lucy Maud Montgomery, "Anne of Green Gables," 1908
Women's Suffrage

World Events/People

First skyscraper in Chicago, 1883
Laura Ingalls Wilder

Core Resources

The Story of Canada
Pages 200-206 – The Last Best West
Pages 207-208 – Dreams and Struggles
Pages 208-210 – A Voice for Women
Pages 210-214 – A Turn-of-the-Century Time Trip
Pages 215-216 – Into the North

My First History of Canada
Chapter 19 – The West God New People (1870-1905)
        Part 1 – First came the cowboys.
        Part 2 – The homesteaders.
        Part 3 – Missionaries gave the Indians a written language.
        Part 4 – New Canadians came from Europe.
            The Mennonites
            The Icelanders
            The Doukhobors
        Part 5 – Wheat made Canada world famous.
        Part 6 – People kept on coming to Canada.
        Part 7 – Alberta and Saskatchewan became provinces.

Flashback Canada
Chapter 28 – Come West
Chapter 29 – Life on a Homestead
Chapter 30 – The Ukranians

A Short History of Canada
Part III – The Century of Canada
        Chapter 2 – Questioning

The Spirit of Canada
Squid-Jiggin' Ground, p. 135
Jack was Every Inch a Sailor, p. 138
Nova Scotia Song, p. 140
First Contact With Canadian Police, p. 143 (Mennonites)
No Flour in the Barrel, p. 149 (Ukranians)
Anne Comes to Green Gables, p. 183
Picking Coke, p. 186
A Secret for Two, p. 187
The Sinking of the Mariposa Belle, p. 241

The Story of the World – Volume 4
Chapter 16 - The Expanding United States
            Moving West
            Stocks, Philanthropists, and Outlaws

Canada: A People's History
Episode 11 – The Great Transformation
        The Last Best West (Immigrants are recruited)
        The Mines and the Minds (Cape Breton mining, Marconi, Silver Dart)
        A Nation of Cities (Industry, urbanization, labour unions)
        A New Map of Canada (Alberta & Saskatchewan created)
        "Fight Fire with Fire" (Women's suffrage)
        Strangers Within Our Gates (Winnipeg, James Shaver Woodsworth)
        Gold Mountain (Asians in British Columbia)

Additional Reading

Westward Ho! 1903 (Cormack, Barbara Villy)
When Jesse Came Across the Sea (Hest, Amy)
Lucy Maud Montgomery (MacLeod, Elizabeth)
Lucy Maud and the Cavendish Cat (Manuel, Lynn)
Maud's House of Dreams: the Life of Lucy Maud Montgomery (Lunn, Janet)
Little House on the Prairie, and other books by Laura Ingalls Wilder
Laura Ingalls Wilder: Author of the Little House Books (Greene, Carol)
Emma and the Silk Train (Lawson, Julie)
Amish Adventure (Smucker, Barbara)
Selena and the Bear Paw Quilt (Smucker, Barbara)
Selena and the Shoo-Fly Pie (Smucker, Barbara)
Treasures of Crazy Quilt Farm (Thum, Marcella)
Ticket to Curlew (Lottridge, Celia)
The Tin-Lined Trunk (Berg, Ron)
John Muir: Man of the Wild Places (Greene, Carol)
Plain Girl (Sorenson, Virginia)
Petranella (Westerton, Betty)
Gully Farm: A Story of Homesteading on the Canadian Prairies (Hiemstra, Mary)
A Prairie Nightmare (Berton, Pierre)

Men in Sheepskin Coats (Berton, Pierre)
Footprints in the Snow, p. 80 (Louis Cyr)
Footprints in the Snow, p. 83 (Ned Hanlan)
Footprints in the Snow, p. 109 (Tekahionwake)
Footprints in the Snow, p. 112 (James Naismith)
Footprints in the Snow, p. 115 (George Dixon)
Footprints in the Snow, p. 117 (Tommy Burns)
Footprints in the Snow, p. 119 (Lucy Maud Montgomery)
Footprints in the Snow, p. 121 (J.A.D. McCurdy & Casey Baldwin)
Footprints in the Snow, p. 125 (Tom Longboat)
Canada Through the Decades: The 1900s (Salomons, Elizabeth)

Part 3 – CANADA IN THE WORLD, THE BOER WAR

Canadian Events/People

Boer War
J.A.D. McCurdy flies the Canadian
Silver Dart (Feb. 1909)

World Events/People

Boer War
Chinese Boxer Rebellion, 1899-1901
Spanish-American War, 1898
Wright Brothers' First Flight (Nov. 1903)

Core Resources

The Story of Canada
Pages 217-219 – The Canadians and the Empire

My First History of Canada
Chapter 20 – Canada in Three Wars (1900-1950)
      Part 1 – Canadians helped Britain in the Boer War

Flashback Canada
      Chapter 31 – At the Turn of the Century
Canada: A Changing Society 1870-1920
      Chapter 32 – The Beginning of Industry
      Chapter 33 – Workers Demand Change

Spotlight Canada
Chapter 4 – Canada – Between Britain and the United States

A History of the English Speaking Peoples – Vol. 4 The Great Democracies
Book XII – The Victorian Age
      Chapter 21 – The South African War

Young People's Story of Our Heritage – The Modern World
      Colonial Expansion

The Story of the World – Volume 4
Chapter 17 - China's Troubles
      The Boxer Rebellion
      The Czar and the Admiral

Canada: A People's History
Episode 11 – The Great Transformation
   For God, Queen and Country (John McCrae, Arms race in Europe)
   "I Am Canadian First" (Supply of warships to Britain)
   Bourassa and the Bishop (French and the Church)
   Attacked From All Sides (Reciprocity, Laurier defeated, Borden elected)

Additional Reading

Usborne World History The Last 500 Years, p. 57 (Boer War)
The Last 500 Years, p. 62-65 (China)
The Last 500 Years, p. 66-67 (Japan)
World Affairs: Defining Canada's Role (Will be useful in the next Unit as well.)
Flying Machine (Eyewitness Book)
The Wright Brothers (Reynolds, Quentin)
The Wright Brothers: A Flying Start (Macleod, Elizabeth)
McCurdy and the Silver Dart (Harding, Les)

Project Ideas

❖ Study the history of one or more of the people groups that immigrated to
   Canada during this time. Several books are suggested above about these
   immigrants. Since we have a Mennonite background, we have several
   books about their origins, such as:

   - The Betrayer's Fortune (Jackson, Dave & Neta)
   - The Secret Church (Vernon, Louise)
   - Night Preacher (Vernon, Louise)
   - Look for books about the history of the Amish people, Ukranians, or
     any other group of your choice.

❖ Compare the Fraser River Gold Rush with the Klondike Gold Rush. How
   did each one affect the formation of Canada? Which had a greater affect
   on Canada?

❖ Visit a pioneer town, preferably one from around the time period of this unit (1880-1910). If you can't visit a town, visit a website! I found a list of historical museums at **www.tinyurl.com/4bcrz** Not all are historical villages, so check each one out before visiting. Some villages from across the country:

- Upper Canada Village (Morrisburg, Ont.) **www.parks.on.ca/village/index.htm**
- Heritage Park Historical Village (Calgary, Alberta) **www.heritagepark.ca/visitor.htm**
- Crowsnest Historical Museum (Crowsnest Pass, Alberta) **www.crowsnestmuseum.ca**
- Fort Edmonton (Edmonton, Alberta) **www.fortedmontonpark.com**
- Ukranian Heritage Village (Edmonton, Alberta) **www.tinyurl.com/5hfv4**
- Doukhobor Village Museum (Castlegar, BC) **www.doukhobor-museum.org**
- Fort Steele Heritage Town (Fort Steele, BC) **www.fortsteele.ca**
- Broken-Beau Pioneer Village Museum (Beausejour, Man) **www.townofbeausejour.com/info/48/broken-beau-pioneer-village-museum**
- Acadian Historical Village (Caraquet, NB) **www.villagehistoriqueacadien.com/main.htm**
- Barbour Living Heritage Village (Newton, Nfld) **www.barbour-site.com**
- Sherbrooke Village (Sherbrooke, NS) **www.museum.gov.ns.ca/sv/index.html**
- Muskoka Heritage Place (Huntsville, Ont) **www.muskokaheritageplace.org/index.html**
- Westfield Heritage Village (Rockton, Ont) **www.westfieldheritage.ca**
- Orwell Corner Historic Village (Orwell, PEI) **www.orwellcorner.isn.net**
- Gaspesian British Heritage Village (New Richmon, Que) **www.villagegaspesien.com**
-

❖ The "Little House" books make great unit studies! There is a lot of information in them about how the settlers of this time period lived. Choose one and try some of the projects found in them. There are study guides and other companion books to help you. Alternatively, just take Laura Ingalls Wilder's description and see what you can do! You could even find small branches and twigs and try making your own miniature homestead house!

❖ A study of the history of aviation might be of interest to some students. My husband, an aerospace engineer with the Canadian Air Force, is intensely interested in this subject, so it is covered in depth in this household! There are many books available about the Wright Brothers, as well as the general history of aviation. If you have a flying fanatic in your house, assign them a project that follows their interest. For all students, it is worthwhile looking at the effect aviation has had on the past hundred years. Aviation is a key advance that has contributed to how small the world is today. Don't forget to go back to Leonardo daVinci's flying machine designs! (See my sketch on page 23 of this guide.) It seems man has always wanted to fly. Why do you suppose that is? How has the invention and development of air travel affected life today? What role did aircraft have in making the world wars different from wars before them? How has aviation made the world smaller in ways other than speed of travel? In the next unit, flying will be dealt with in greater detail, but this is a good time to note the beginnings of this important field.

World Connection

- ❖ Research the Boer War. What was the war about? What events led to the war? Which party in the war do you think was right? Do you think Canada was right to take part in the war? Keep in mind that wars, like most things in life, are not as simple as they may sound in one brief textbook recounting. This would be a good project for a high school essay, and could lead to an essay on the merits/pitfalls of world involvement.

- ❖ Write an essay about how the Boer War affected Canada's role in the world. Would our role in WWI have been different if we had chosen not to participate in the Boer War? Did the Boer War somehow prepare us as a nation for world involvement? How did these events help shape Canadians' views on world involvement? In what way has Canada's policy on world involvement changed since the Boer War and the World Wars?

- ❖ Research life in Europe during the period of 1880-1915. Compare and contrast it with life in Canada during the same time. Consider all aspects of life - dress, food, housing, social activities, music, art, etc.

- ❖ Research the Spanish-American War and/or the Chinese Boxer Rebellion to gain a bigger picture of the world during this time.

UNIT 9 – THE TWENTIETH CENTURY BELONGS TO CANADA!

The history in this unit is beginning to feel closer to the present day. There are those still living who remember what we will study in this unit. They are your most valuable resource - be sure not to overlook the riches of their memories. My mother remembers her favorite uncle going to war; and coming home again after the war. She remembers the parade through town as the men marched gloriously home, and the joy of their return. She also remembers the fear waiting for that day. These kinds of memories bring history alive. They remind us of where we've been so we can better understand where we are. It also reminds us of God's faithfulness, thereby urging us to keep trusting Him. My in-laws' parents escaped persecution in Russia between the two world wars. Their story is remarkable and I am glad it has been preserved to pass down to my children. This is in direct obedience to God's command to the Israelites in Deuteronomy 6 to teach our children what He has done for us so they will always know of His faithfulness.

The events in these units might not have directly involved your family members, but they are the events that have shaped our country and so have great relevance for us all. I hope through the units I have inspired you to make history personal - to sink your teeth in and get to know the people who have made our world what it is today.

When studying a subject as controversial as war, beware of books with a blatant "pro-war" or "anti-war" worldview. Some books are written with the purpose of convincing the reader of the rightness or wrongness of an issue, but are cleverly designed as a novel or factual history book. These books can still be useful, as long as you are aware of the author's worldview and discuss your own beliefs about such things as war with your children and/or read this type of book along with them. It can also be a good exercise in teaching children to discern facts from opinion and interpretation of facts. History is replete with issues of which this is true, war being one of the more obvious ones.

Whatever your personal views are, be sure to give this unit the time and depth of study that it deserves. We have seen how Canada struggled to survive and become a country in her own right, and now we are finally going to see what she did with that identity. Canada has been an infant, a newly discovered country; a child, setting up colonies and defining her borders; and a young adult, striking out on her own, writing her own constitution, making her own laws. Now Canada is like that young adult after she has discovered who she is: She is now free to return home and help, not as a child, but as a partner. Canada is now going to stand up and be counted in her own right in the world. Sir Wilfrid Laurier knew this when he said that the 20th century belongs to Canada!

Part 1 – THE FIRST WORLD WAR

Canadian Events/People

World War I
Sir Robert Laird Borden
Billy Bishop
Billy Barker

World Events/People

World War I
Russian Revolution
Lenin
Albert Einstein (Theory of Relativity – 1915)

Core Resources

The Story of Canada
Pages 222 – 223 – Stormy Times
Pages 223-226 – Trench Warfare
Pages 226-230 – Struggles at Home

My First History of Canada
Chapter 20, part 2 – After the First World War Canada became a nation.

The Spirit of Canada
The Wars, p. 192
In Flanders Fields, p. 193
Our Dugout, p. 195

<u>Canada: A People's History</u>
Episode 11 – The Great Transformation
       "It Will Be a Terrible War" (WWI begins)
Episode 12 – Ordeal by Fire (1915-1929)
       (Enlistment)
       "Our Investment of Blood" (prohibition, women get the vote)
       The Spoils of War (Business and industry of war)
       The Battle of Vimy Ridge
       City of Sorrow (Halifax explosion)
       A Broken Promise (Conscription question)
       A Painful Peace (Armistice, veterans, League of Nations)

Additional Reading

The Kids' Book of Canadian Prime Ministers
In Flanders Fields: The Story of the Poem by John McCrae (Granfield, Linda)
Kids' Book of Canadian History, "World War 1" p. 52
Kids' Book of Canadian Prime Ministers, p. 23 (Robert Borden)
Footprints in the Snow, p. 134 (Soldiers' Medals)
Footprints in the Snow, p. 137 (Billy Bishop)
Footprints in the Snow, p. 138 (Billy Barker)
Footprints in the Snow, p. 141 ("Wop" May)
Rilla of Ingleside (Montgomery, Lucy Maud)
Goodbye Sarah (Bilson, Geoffrey)
Days of Terror (Smucker, Barbara)
The Halifax Disaster (Robinson, Ernest Fraser)
In Flanders Fields (Granfield, Linda)
Knights of the Air (Harris, John Norman)
Knights of the Air: Canadian Fighter Pilots in the First World War (Bashow, David)
Invitation to the Classics – James Joyce (p. 307-310)
Great Canadian Political Cartoons (Hou, Charles and Cynthia)
World War I - History of Warfare Series (Sommerville, Donald)
Canada Through the Decades: The 1910s (Craats, Rennay)
Biggles series (Captain W.E. Johns)

Part 2 – THE ROARING TWENTIES AND THE DIRTY THIRTIES

Canadian Events/People

Frederick Banting
Tom Thompson
The Group of Seven
Emily Murphy
Nellie McClung

World Events/People

Marie Curie (1867-1934)
Thomas Edison (1847-1931)
Gandhi

Core Resources

The Story of Canada
Pages 231-235 – The Heartbreaking Twenties
Pages 235-240 – The Dirty Thirties
Pages 240-241 – Escaping from the Bad Times

My First History of Canada
Chapter 20 part 3 – Then came the boom.
       Part 4 – The bush pilots opened up the great northland.
       Part 5 – When the boom burst.

Flashback Canada
Chapter 34 – Workers and The Winnipeg General Strike
Chapter 35 – Alternative Ways to Change
Chapter 36 – Women Demand Change
Chapter 37 – Only the Beginning
Chapter 38 – Farmers Demand Change

The Spirit of Canada
The Dirty Thirties, p. 202
Flunky Jim, p. 203
The Coming of Mutt, p. 204
Saskatchewan, p. 210

Spotlight Canada
Chapter 8 – Moving Into the Twenties
Chapter 9 – Life in the Roaring Twenties
Chapter 10 – The Great Crash
Chapter 11 – Life in the Dirty Thirties

A Short History of Canada
Part III – The Century of Canada
        Chapter 4 – Dead Ends
        Chapter 5 – The Depression

Canadian History for Dummies
Chapter 18 – The Dirty Thirties

Young People's Story of Our Heritage – The Modern World
        Boom, Depression, and Revolution

The Story of the World – Volume 4
Chapter 24 - The King and Il Duce
                The First King of Egypt
                Fascism in Italy
Chapter 25 - Armies in China
                Japan, China, and a Pretend Emperor
                The Long March
Chapter 26 - The Great Crash, and What Came of It
                Black Tuesday and a New Deal
                Hitler's Rise to Power

Concise Historical Atlas of Canada
Plate 16 – Migration, 1891-1930
Plate 21 – The Emergence of the Urban System, 1888-1932
Plate 26 – Primary Production, 1891-1926
Plate 28 – The Changing Structure of Manufacturing, 1879-1930
Plate 33 – Religious Adherence, 20th Century
Plate 41 – The Impact of the Great Depression, 1930s
Plate 58 – The Emergence of Corporate Toronto, 1890-1930
Plate 62 – Peopling the Prairies, 1891-1931
Plate 63 – Drought and Depression on the Prairies, 1930s
Plate 65 – British Columbia Resources, 1891-1928
Plate 66 – Resource Development on the Shield, 1891-1928

Canada: A People's History
Episode 12 – Ordeal by Fire
       The Winnipeg General Strike
       We'll Hoe Our Own Row (Agnes McPhail, Farmers unions, Mackenzie King)
       "At the Mercy of Our Neighbours" (American economic influence, stock market crash)

Episode 13 – Hard Times (1929-1940)
       (Depression, drought)
       Descent Into Chaos ("The Dole," Joey Smallwood)
       An Era Being Born (Jazz)
       The Enemies Within (Joseph Stalin, Communist threat in Canada)
       Needles and Pins (Factory conditions, J.D. Eaton)
       Blown Away (Prairie conditions)
       Dear Mr. Prime Minister
       The End of the Line ("On to Ottawa" trek, King re-elected)
       A Clean Sweep (Provincial leaders, Social Credit)
       A League of Her Own (Carine Wilson, Fascism)
       The Politics of Hope (Cooperative Commonwealth Federation)
       Love and War (Civil war in Spain, Foreign Enlistment Act)
       The Grip Tightens (Maurice Duplessis)

Additional Reading

The Kids' Book of Canadian History, "Changing Times" p. 53
Footprints in the Snow, p. 146 (Agnes Campbell Macphail)
Footprints in the Snow, p. 148 (Frederick Banting)
Footprints in the Snow, p. 152 (Tom Thomson)
Footprints in the Snow, p. 155 (Percy Page)
Footprints in the Snow, p. 157 (George Yong)
Footprints in the Snow, p. 160 (Bobbie Rosenfeld)
Footprints in the Snow, p. 163 (Ethel Catherwood)
Footprints in the Snow, p. 164 (Emile St. Godard)
Footprints in the Snow, p. 166 (Howie Morenz)
Footprints in the Snow, p. 168 (Grey Owl)
Footprints in the Snow, p. 172 (Dr. Norman Bethune)
Footprints in the Snow, p. 182 (Earl McCready)
Footprints in the Snow, p. 184 (Armand Bombardier)
Footprints in the Snow, p. 186 (Colonel Dan)
Footprints in the Snow, p. 188 (Emily Carr)
Footprints in the Snow, p. 192 (Lionel Conacher)
The Dog Who Wouldn't Be (Mowat, Farley)
Marie Curie: Pioneer Physicist (Greene, Carol)
Defeat of the Ghost Riders (Jackson, Dave & Neta)
The Dust Bowl (Booth, David)
Thomas Alva Edison: Bringer of Light (Greene, Carol)

As for Me and My House (Ross, Sinclair)
Frederick G. Banting: The Discoverer of Insulin (Levine, I.E.)
Rose's Journal: The Story of a Girl in the Great Depression (Moss, Marissa)
Thomas Edison (Gaines, Ann) (gr. 2-3)
Invitation to the Classics – Franz Kafka (p. 311-314)
Invitation to the Classics – William Butler Yeats (p. 315-318)
Invitation to the Classics – T.S. Eliot (p. 319-322)
Invitation to the Classics – Robert Frost (p. 323-326)
Canada Through the Decades: The 1920s (Baldwin, Douglas)
Canada Through the Decades: The 1930s (Baldwin, Douglas)

Part 3 – THE SECOND WORLD WAR

Canadian Events/People

World War II
William Lyon Mackenzie King

World Events/People

World War II
Winston Churchill

Core Resources

The Story of Canada
Pages 241-245 – War Again
Pages 245-247 – At Sea and in the Air
Pages 247-254 – On the Home Front
Pages 254-255 – The End of the War

My First History of Canada
Chapter 20, part 6 – The Second World War.
        Part 7 – The years after the war brought many new Canadians.
        Part 8 – Newfoundland joined Canada.

The Spirit of Canada
High Flight, p. 196
This Was My Brother, p. 197
A Child in Prison Camp, p. 198

Spotlight Canada
Chapter 12 – The Rise of the Nazi Dictator
Chapter 18 – The War in Europe and the Pacific
Chapter 19 – Total War

A Short History of Canada
Part IV – Middle Age, Middle Power
        Chapter 1 – Mr. King's War

Canadian History for Dummies
Chapter 19 – World War II

Young People's Story of Our Heritage – The Modern World
        World War II
        Allied Victories

Additional Reading

Kids' Book of Canadian History, "World War II" p. 56
Kids' Book of Canadian Prime Ministers, p. 25 (Arthur Meighen)
Kids' Book of Canadian Prime Ministers, p. 26 (William Lyon Mackenzie King)
Kids' Book of Canadian Prime Ministers, p. 31 (Richard Bedford Bennett)
Footprints in the Snow, p. 178 ("Buzz" Beurling)
Footprints in the Snow, p. 180 (Johnny Longden)
Footprints in the Snow, p. 190 (Barbara Ann Scott)
Footprints in the Snow, p. 195 (Brock Chisholm)
Footprints in the Snow, p. 197 (Doug Hepburn)
Ultra Hush-hush: Espionage and Special Missions (Shapiro, Stephen) (gr. 5-8)
Those Incredible Women of World War II (Zeinert, Karen) (gr. 5-8)
Life of a Nazi Soldier (Cartlidge, Cherese) (high school)
Invitation to the Classics – C.S. Lewis (p. 335-338)
Invitation to the Classics – William Faulkner (p. 339-344)
Invitation to the Classics – Deitrich Bonhoeffer (p. 349-352)
Dr. Seuss Goes to War: The World War II Editorial Cartoons of Theodor Seuss Geisel (Minear, Richard H.)
World War II - History of Warfare Series (Sharpe, Mike)
Canada Through the Decades: The 1940s (Craats, Rennay)
The Zion Chronicles (Series by Thoene, Bodie)
The Exodus (movie starring Paul Newman and Eva Marie Saint)
Biggles series (Captain W.E. Johns)

Project Ideas

❖ A good historical atlas is essential to this study. Any historical atlas covering the 20th century will have maps of the world wars and battles that were fought. The <u>Concise Historical Atlas of Canada</u> (edited by William G. Dean, et al) has several. The benefit to this atlas is that it indicates on these maps where Canadian troops fought, as well as which units. If you do not have this atlas, I highly recommend you request it from your library for this unit. If you have a friend or relative who fought in the war, find out what unit they were with and you can track where they fought!

❖ Shortly before we moved from Ottawa we visited the National War Museum, and we are very glad we did! It is an exceptional field trip at any time during a study of Canadian History, as the museum covers Canada's military history right from the beginning. If you live close enough, you may find several trips during your study to be useful and interesting. However, if you can only go once, it would be most beneficial to go during your study of the two world wars. The War Museum is one of the most educationally informative museums I have attended. I highly recommend this field trip. If you are not able to visit the museum in person, and even if you are, check out the web site: **www.warmuseum.ca/cwm/cwme.asp** It includes many essays and informative pages on specific events in our military history, as well as a list of outside links.

❖ If you want to do a project on the First World War, a great website with lots of information is **www.worldwar1.com**. Even with nothing particularly Canadian on this site, it is still a very informative site about WWI. It includes a detailed timeline, maps, trench maps, biographies, memoirs, and much more. A web site with information on WWI from the Canadian perspective is **www.collectionscanada.ca/firstworldwar/index-e.html.html**. This page includes war diaries, short biographies of those who fought in the war, and more. It also has some interesting extras such as the "Now you be the historian" section. For World War II have a look at **www.wwii.ca**. This site has lots of information, including some rather challenging quizzes. You'll find a detailed timeline of WWII at **www.news.bbc.co.uk/onthisday/hi/themes/conflict_and_war/world_war_ii/default.stm** For teacher's resources for both wars, go to **www.virtualmuseum.ca/English/Teacher/world_war.html**

❖ The Aviation Museum, also in Ottawa, is another wonderful resource. The development of aviation played a major role in both world wars, and this museum has everything from a replica Silver Dart (the first Canadian plane) to the only remaining piece (the nose) of an Avro Arrow, to a recently retired CF-18 fighter jet. (This CF-18 is so recent that my husband has flown in it!) Well-informed guides are always on hand to answer questions. Their website is **www.aviation.technomuses.ca** and is full of great information.

❖ There are some excellent articles on WWI in the summer 2004 issue of Airforce Magazine. You can find this publication at **www.airforce.ca** for subscription purposes, but you cannot read articles on-line. If your local library does not carry this magazine, a local Royal Canadian Legion is sure to have it and/or other informative magazines and articles.

❖ Visit a military base near you. Most have areas that are open to the public, and offer tours of their facilities. Every Squadron has memorabilia from each war they fought in. My husband's squadron proudly displays a Nazi flag which they captured during WWII. Base personnel are always happy to talk to those who are interested in learning about Canada's military history! You might even be able to arrange a tour for your local homeschool group.

❖ If you decide to do some studying about Canada's military history, either with your older student or on your own, an excellent book on the subject is A Military History of Canada: From Champlain to Kosovo, by Desmond Morton. I found it to be a good, solid history of Canada, even though it focuses on the military side of things. The history of a nation is greatly shaped by the military activity it is involved in, so knowing the military history of a country helps one to round out their knowledge of the nation's history. The author is very good at sticking with the facts without letting his own personal biases show.

❖ Talk to your relatives! I realize this time period is moving farther and farther into our past, but anyone born before 1940 should have some recollection of WWII. Those born earlier may remember life during the Great Depression. If you have no relatives or friends from that era, visit a senior's home and make a friend! There is bound to be someone who would just love to help your child with a school project by telling stories from their youth. Another wonderful resource is the local Royal Canadian Legion. There you should find men and women who served in WWII and who would love to talk to you about it. Another idea is to attend a Remembrance Day ceremony. Just attending will be a great experience to enrich your study of the world wars, but there are bound to be people there who would be more than willing to talk to you. You can always identify them by their uniform or their Legion blazer.

❖ Attend an air show. Lots of information on the history of aviation can be found at air shows. The larger ones generally have military aircraft, making it a great place to learn some military history as well. The annual Abbotsford Airshow (usually held in early August) is the largest in Canada.

World Connection

❖ The predominant events in the world during this time were the two world wars. Since these wars were important in Canada's history as well, it is easy to see how the world affected Canada during this time. It is also important to note that Canada began to affect the world around her as well. Taking each of the wars separately, study the causes of each, why each country became involved, and the effect of the war on each of the individual countries involved.

❖ Choose one or two countries that were involved in the war (do this for one or both wars) and research in more detail the affect the war had on that country as well as how that country influenced the result of the war.

❖ Choose one or more battles that the Canadians were involved in to study in more depth. Gather all the statistics and write an essay answering the question of how the Canadians impacted the outcome of the battle, and what role that battle had in the overall war.

❖ Compare and contrast the two wars with respect to one or more of the following topics:
   - life as a soldier
   - weaponry
   - impact on civilian life
   - Canadian perspective/support
   - world leaders involved
   - what was at stake?
   - how the war changed the landscape (political/geographic results)

❖ It is amazing what one can find using Google.com! I happened across some lesson plans for World War 1 history. There are charts and information giving more details about who was who and what part they played. You can find these lessons at **www.spartacus.schoolnet.co.uk/TGfww.htm**

UNIT 10 - POST WAR PRESENT DAY CANADA

Congratulations! We have made it to the final unit of our Canadian History study! This unit covers many years, years that most of us remember as current events. So take your time. If you want a brief overview, you could certainly cover this unit in one month, but if you want a more thorough study, it would be better to spread it out over 2 or more months. Depending on the depth with which you want to cover the material, you could even spend one month per section.

There are many resources available for this period. But remember: The most interesting resource is someone who has been there. In this unit, particularly the latter part of it, that someone is you! Talk to your children about the events you remember and how each affected you and your family. Have your children talk to their grandparents or other people you know to hear about earlier events first hand. History is so much more exciting when viewed through the eyes of those who were there! Some of the recent events your children may even remember themselves. Remind them of that. This could very easily lead into a study of current events, if you don't already follow current events with your children. Move from the 90's section right into the new millennium and check the local paper to see what is happening this week! My daughter has decided to take her time line into the future by adding newspaper clippings to it as things happen. I think this is a wonderful idea! Not only does this help students to be aware of what's going on in the world around them, but it also helps them to understand that history is really just "current events" that have already happened.

Remember also that history is always filtered through the viewer's worldview. I found in most of the resources that the authors' worldviews were evident in their writing, even though they may have tried to balance it, more in this chapter than in any other. Of course, it will always seep through to some degree because that is how we process information and how we interpret it. It is important to keep that in mind as you read the resources, and to edit, or interpret, the information for your children with the worldview that you are shaping in them. There are paragraphs that require significant editing/interpretation when reading with my older children, and may be skipped altogether when I read them with my younger children.

Once you complete your study of Canadian History, you may want to embark on a unit of Canadian Geography, learning all the Provincial and Territorial capitals, economic regions and geographic landmarks, etc. if you have not done so through your history study. Additionally, if your children are older, you may want to do a study on Canadian Government. I have listed some resources at the end of this guide to get your started on those ventures.

I hope you have enjoyed our journey through Canadian History as much as I have. It is exciting to look back and see where we have come from as a people, but even more exciting to see how our past affects the people we will become in the future.

Part 1 - THE 50s

Canadian Events/People

Louis Stephen St. Laurent (PM 1948-57)
John George Diefenbaker (PM 1957-63)
Farley Mowat
Newfoundland becomes a Province (1949)
Avro Arrow (1959)
Marilyn Bell crosses the English Channel (1954)

World Events/People

Korean War (1950-53)
Formation of NATO
Formation of the United Nations (1945)

Core Resources

The Story of the World – Volume 4
Chapter 31 - Western Bullies and American Money
          The Suez Crisis
          The Marshall Plan
Chapter 32 - Africa and China After World War II
          One Country, Two Different Worlds
          Two Republics of China
Chapter 33 - Communism in Asia
          Ho Chi Minh and the Viet Minh
          The Korean War
Chapter 34 - Dictators in South America and Africa
          Argentina's President and His Wife
          Freedom in the Belgian Congo

Canada: A People's History
Episode 15 – Comfort and Fear (1946-1964)
     (Refugees)
     From Sea to Sea (Newfoundland joins Confederation)
     "Refus Global" (Quebec cultural changes, strikes, Maurice Duplessis)
     Boom (Oil in Alberta, other natural resources)
     Seeing Red (NATO, Korea, Cold War, Communist threat)
     Affluence for Almost All (Construction boom, CBC)
     "On Guard for Thee" (Defence in the North, Lester Pearson)
     First Tremors (Affluence, Rocket Richard, Elvis)
Canada: A People's History (continued)
     A Prairie Storm (Diefenbaker AB-Ont pipeline, American economic
     involvement)
     The Crossroads (Media influence, Canadian media, Quebec strike)
     Shifting Symbols (St. Lawrence Seaway, Joyce Davidson)
     "Time for Change" (Réne Lévesque, seperatism)
     The Fight for Medicare (Tommy Douglas)
     The Shadow of Nuclear War (NORAD, Avro Arrow/Bomark Missle)

Additional Reading

The Last 500 Years, p. 84-86, 96-97
Kids' Book of Canadian History, p. 58-59
Kids' Book of Canadian Prime Ministers, p. 33-36
Footprints in the Snow, p. 199 (Marilyn Bell)
The Bells on Finland Street (Cook, Lyn)
Race for the Record: Joy Ridderhof (Jackson, Dave & Neta)
The Fate of the Yellow Woodbee: Nate Saint (Jackson, Dave & Neta)
Avro Arrow (Organ, Richard)
The Arrow (Video/DVD starring Dan Ackroyd)
Owls in the Family (Mowat, Farley) and other books by Farley Mowat
Introducing Farley Mowat: A Selection From His Works (Mowat, Farley)
The Farley Mowat Reader (Mowat, Farley) – excerpts from his works

Shooting Hoops and Skating Loops: Great Inventions in Sports (Hegedus, Alannah)

Canada Invents! (Hughes, Susan)

Invitation to the Classics – Simone Weil (p. 345-348)

Invitation to the Classics – Flannery O'Connor (p. 353-356)

Warfare in the Modern World – History of Warfare Series (Grant, R.G.)

Canada Through the Decades: The 1950s (Hacker, Carlotta)

Elvis

50's

P. M. Diefenbaker

CBC T. V.

War Brides

Avrow Arrow

115

Part 2 - THE 60's

Canadian Events/People

Lester Bowles Pearson (PM
1963-68)
Maple Leaf Flag adopted (1965)
Rene Levesque
DC8 flies Vancouver to Toronto
in 5 hours (1960)
Pierre Berton
Glenn Gould

World Events/People

Neil Armstrong, first man on
moon (1969)
Martin Luther King (1963)
Beetles come to Canada (1963)
Cold War begins
Woodstock (1969)

Core Resources

The Story of Canada
Pages 272-276 – "Il faut que ça change!"
Pages 276-280 – Canada's Birthday Party

My First History of Canada
Chapter 21, part 3 – Canada gets a flag and an anthem.
   Part 4 – Canada has a big birthday party.
   Part 5 – Canada develops her natural and human resources.
   Part 6 – Problems and opportunities.

The Spirit of Canada
How Canada Got Its Flag, p. 213
CA-NA-DA, p. 214
The Centennial Train, p. 215
Mon Pays, p. 224
Something to Sing About, p. 268

Spotlight Canada
Chapter 17 – The Swinging Sixties

A Short History of Canada
Part IV – Middle Age, Middle Power
   Chapter 4 - Confusion

Canadian History for Dummies
Chapter 21 – The Battle For Quebec

The Story of the World – Volume 4
Chapter 35 - The Cold War
            The Space Race
            Thirteen Days in October
Chapter 36 - Struggles and Assassinations
            The Death of John F. Kennedy
            Civil Rights

Concise Historical Atlas of Canada
Plate 11 – Territorial Evolution, 1891-1961
Plate 17 – Population Changes, 1941-1961
Plate 18 – Population Composition, 1891-1961
Plate 22 – The Integration of the Urban System, 1921-1961
Plate 23 – The Growth of Road and Air Transport, 20th Century
Plate 27 – Farming and Fishing, 1941-1961
Plate 67 – Societies and Economies in the North, 1891-1961

World Atlas of the Past
Pages 40-43 – Russia in the 20th CenturyRussia
Pages 44-47 – Asia Since 1945

Canada: A People's History
Episode 16 – Years of Hope and Anger (1964-1976)
        (Folk music, nationalism)
        Maîtres Chez Nous (Education reform in Quebec)
        The Planners of Happiness (W.A.C. Bennett, Joey Smallwood, relocation, redevelopment)
        A Question of Equality (Women at work, birth control, abortion)
        Under a New Flag (Bilingualism, new flag)
        Going Down the Road (moving from Newfoundland)

Additional Reading

The Last 500 Years (Usborne), p. 88-91, 94-95
Kids' Book of Canadian History, p. 60-61
Kids' Book of Canadian Prime Ministers, p. 37-38
Footprints in the Snow, p. 200 (Two Famous Canadian Ships)
Footprints in the Snow, p. 202 (Nancy Green)
Footprints in the Snow, p. 205 (Lester B. Pearson)
Jacques Cousteau: Man of the Oceans (Greene, Carol)
The Secret World of Og (Berton, Pierre) and other books by Pierre Berton
Struggling for Perfection: The Story of Glenn Gould (Konieczny, Vladimir)
Invitation to the Classics – Aleksandr I. Solzhenitsyn (p. 357-360)
Canada Through the Decades: The 1960s (Shipton, Rosemary)

peace!

Canada Centennial

Lester Pearson

DELICIOUS REFRESHING

60's Slang

Slang Term	Meaning
Bread	Money
Rap	discuss
Groovy	really fine
Flower child	hippie
Far out	great!
Out of sight	terrific!
Good vibes	positive feelings

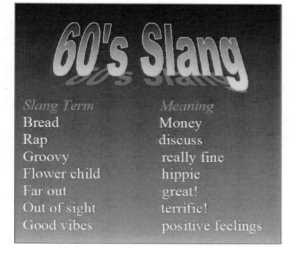

Part 3 - THE 70's

Canadian Events/People

Pierre Elliott Trudeau (PM 1968-79, 1980-84)
Charles Joseph Clark (PM 1979-80)
Bilingualism
FLQ Kidnapping (1970)
Paul Henderson's goal (1972)
Greenpeace Founded (1971)

World Events/People

Nixon and Watergate Scandal (1974)
US Viking probe lands on Mars (1976)
Margaret Thatcher (becomes PM of England 1979)
Vietnam War

Core Resources

The Story of Canada
Pages 280-282 – Coming Together – Flying Apart
Pages 282-283 – Battle of the Titans
Pages 283-288 – Energy and Ecology

The Spirit of Canada
Why Can't We Talk to Each Other? p. 218
Song for Canada, p. 222

Spotlight Canada
Chapter 18 – Canada and Quebec: One Nation or Two?
Chapter 19 – Canada, The United States, and the World

A Short History of Canada
Part V – A Country Shared
        Chapter 1 – Liberation
        Chapter 2 – Affirmation

Canadian History for Dummies
Chapter 22 – A Charter Country

The Story of the World – Volume 4
Chapter 37 - Two Short Wars and One Long One
                The Vietnam War
                Trouble in the Middle East
Chapter 38 - Two Ways of Fighting
                Soviet Invasions
                Terrorism

World Atlas of the Past
Pages 52-55 – The World by 1975

Canada: A People's History
Episode 16 – Years of Hope and Anger
        Vive le Quebec Libre (Charles de Gaul, Trudeau)
        Do Your Own Thing (Youth culture, FLQ, Vietnam War, Greenpeace)
        Taking Back the Past (Native policies)
        Language Wars (Official Languages Act)
        October 1970 (FLQ kidnappings)
        A Most Fundamental Choice (Royal Commission on Women,
        Morgentaller)
        The End of Illusions (Paul Henderson, Quebec strike, War in Middle East)
        A Winning Strategy (Réne Lévesque, Parti Quebecois, Referendum)

Additional Reading

The Last 500 Years (Usborne), p. 98-99
The Kids' Book of Canadian History, p. 62-65
The Kids' Book of Canadian Prime Ministers, p. 39-44
Assassins in the Cathedral: Festo Kivengere (Jackson, Dave & Neta)
Canada Through the Decades: The 1970s (Craats, Rennay)

Part 4 – THE 80s

Canadian Events/People

John Napier Turner (PM June-Sept. 1984)
Martin Brian Mulroney (PM 1984-93)
Marc Garneau, first Canadian in Space (1984)
Terry Fox (1980)
Rick Hansen (1986)
Meech Lake Accord (1987)
Reform Party Formed (1987)

World Events/People

Gorbachev (1984)
Berlin Wall crumbles

Core Resources

The Story of Canada
Pages 289-291 – Lean and Mean
Pages 291-292 – Living in the 1980s
Pages 292-295 – The Global Village

A Short History of Canada
Part V – A Country Shared
        Chapter 3 - Individualism

Canadian History for Dummies
Chapter 23 – "Yankee Doodle Dandy;" The Mulroney Years

The Story of the World – Volume 4
Chapter 39 - The 1980s in the East and the Mideast
                India After Partition
                Iran and Iraq
Chapter 40 - The 1980s in the USSR
                Chernobyl and Nuclear Power
                The End of the Cold War
Chapter 41 - Communism Crumbles – but Survives
                Democracy in China?
                Communism Crumbles

<u>Canada: A People's History</u>
Episode 17 – In An Uncertain World (1976 – 1990)
     (Oil boom in Alberta, National Energy Program)
     The Choice (Quebec sovereignty referendum)
     Hard Times (Recession)
     Solidarity (Bill Bennet, general strike)
     "The Night of the Long Knives" (Patriation of the Constitution, Charter of Rights)
     "The World Was Mine" (Charter of Rights, Feminism)
     A Changing Face (Immigrants)
     The Computer Moves In
     From the Ground Up (Environmentalism)
     Land and Nation (Aboriginal land claims, Oka)
     "Honour and Enthusiasm" (Meech Lake Accord)
     Winners and Losers (Free Trade)

Additional Reading

The Last 500 Years (Usborne), p. 92-92, 100-101
Kids' Book of Canadian History, p. 66-69
Kids' Book of Canadian Prime Ministers, p. 45-49
Elie Weisel: Messenger from the Holocaust (Greene, Carol)
Terry Fox: His Story (Scrivener, Leslie)
Rick Hansen: Man in Motion (Hansen, Rick)
Best Canadian Political Cartoons 1984 (Stahl, N.M.)
Chins and Needles: Political Cartoons (Donato, Andy)
Donato's 1980 Political Cartoons (Donato, Andy)
Canada Through the Decades: The 1980s (Parker, Janice)

Part 5 - THE 90's AND BEYOND!

Canadian Events/People

Avril Kim Campbell (PM June-Nov 1993)
Joseph Jacques Jean Cretien (PM 1993-2003)
Paul Martin (PM 2003-present)
Lucien Buchard (1994)
Charlottetown Accord (1992)
Separatism Referendum (1995)

World Events/People

The Persian Gulf War (1990-1991)
Nelson Mandela (1994)
Space Station (2000)
Terrorists fly into the World Trade Centre (Sept 11, 2001)
War on Terror (2001+)

Core Resources

The Story of Canada
Page 296-300 – First Nations and Distinct Societies

The Spirit of Canada
Wild Pitch, p. 256 (Blue Jays win the World Series in 1992)
I Am A Canadian, p. 290

Spotlight Canada
Chapter 20 – Canada: A Nation of Diversity and Change

A Short History of Canada
Part V – A Country Shared
        Chapter 4 – Paying the Price
        Chapter 5 – New Choices

Canadian History for Dummies
Chapter 24 – Where Do We Go From Here?

Young People's Story of Our Heritage – The Modern World
        Yesterday, Today, and Tomorrow

The Story of the World – Volume 4
Chapter 42 - The End of the Twentieth Century
        The First Persian Gulf War
        Africa, Independent

<u>World Atlas of the Past</u>
Pages 48-51 – The Middle East Since 1948
Pages 56-59 – The World Today

Additional Reading

The Last 500 Years, p. 86-87, 102-103
Kids' Book of Canadian Prime Ministers, p. 50-52
The Killick (Butler, Geoff)
Fog Cat (Helmer, Marily)
Blinded by the Shining Path: Romulo Saune (Jackson, Dave & Neta)
Canada Through the Decades: The 1990s (Seidlitz, Lauri)

Project Ideas

❖ Choose a topic from each decade, or just focus on one or two, to dig into more deeply. For example, the history of hockey and/or the NHL, Canadian athletes in the world, the making and destruction of the Avro Arrow, Canada in Space (Marc Garneau, the Canadarm, etc), Canada in the Korean War or Canada in the Gulf War, etc. Let your interests guide you!

❖ Choose a Canadian from this time period who deserves the title "hero." Explain why this person is heroic in your view, and how he or she may not have been heroic.

❖ Greenpeace began in British Columbia, but it has affected more than its own corner of the world. Research its origins and its goals. Explain both the benefits and the drawbacks of the environmentalist views.

❖ Research the development of the Avro Arrow and why the program was cancelled. This is a fascinating story of Canadian skill and tenacity in the face of tremendous opposition. Find out where the team members who worked on the Arrow project went after the project was cancelled and the impact they have had on the aviation and space industries. What could have happened to the Canadian aviation industry if they had been allowed to complete the Arrow and continue working together at the Avro Company? Consider the effects on the Canadian economy and also on Canada's place in the world in terms of the aviation market and defense.

World Connection

❖ How did Canada affect the world of the 20th Century? Using examples, explain how we have contributed to the world at large.

❖ Research the rise and fall of Communism. Why did it rise in the first place? What were the benefits? How did it sustain itself? What ultimately led to its downfall? Are the countries that were part of the USSR better off now that they are independent? Explain why or why not.

❖ Many advances have been made in the space industry in the last 60 years. Research Canada's role in these advances. Read a biography of Neil Armstrong. How would it feel to be the first person to set foot on the moon? Write a short story about the experience. Do some artwork based on the space theme. Some wonderful effects can be made with white chalk on black construction paper.

❖ Research Canada's involvement in recent world conflicts. What type of involvement did Canada have? What factors affect how Canada is involved in world events?

❖ There is great debate in the world over the current war in Iraq. Research the war and have a debate with a sibling or friend about the war. Remember to stick to provable facts in your argument. Debates should never become emotional!

❖ Many conflicts have taken place in history, and in recent years, between Israel and the Palestinians. In fact, these two people groups have been at odds ever since their beginnings in Abraham's sons, Isaac and Ishmael. Research the history of the conflict. Go back to Biblical times and write an essay about the beginnings of the people and their conflict. Relate it to today's struggles. Why do these two groups have such a difficult time getting along? What are some of the conflicts that they struggle over? How does this relate to their history? Can we properly evaluate these conflicts without understanding their Biblical past? Some excellent resources for following current conflicts are The Jerusalem Post (**www.jpost.com**) and The Ha'aretz (**www.haaretz.com**)

GEOGRAPHY RESOURCES

* ❖ <u>Explore Canada Through Maps</u> (by George Williams, Published by Apple Press Publishing) – This is a wonderful hands-on study of maps for older primary students up to the middle school level. My grade 2 and 4 students both enjoyed it immensely.

* ❖ <u>The Big Book of Canada: Exploring the Provinces and Territories</u> (by Christopher Moore) - A fun look at Canada's diverse land for all ages. Geographical, economic and cultural facts, plus information on famous people from each region.

* ❖ <u>Journey Through Canada</u> (by Richard Tames) - A very brief overview of the land we call Canada. Not my favourite, but good for a quick peek at what Canada holds.

* ❖ <u>Canada Colouring Book</u> – Great for elementary age students.

* ❖ <u>Symbols of Canada</u> (Published by Canadian Heritage) – A beautiful, glossy page book, explaining all kinds of Canadian symbols, as well as provincial symbols. (Flags, coats of arms, birds, flowers, etc.) There is a lot more information in this book than I expected!

* ❖ <u>Contact Canada</u> (Oxford University Press) – Upper Middle School to High School level. A traditional style Geography text. Lots of detailed information and geography skills will be found in this book!

CANADIAN GOVERNMENT RESOURCES

❖ Spotlight Canada
  - Chapter 21 – Government – It's All Around Us
  - Chapter 22 – Law and Citizenship.

❖ Web sites of the various political parties. Don't take the word of one author about what any one party believes. They will almost always unintentionally misrepresent all parties but their own. Go to the source and read the parties' own policy statements.

❖ How Canada Got Its Capital (National Capital Commission) – In story form, this would make a great read-aloud with younger children. Students in grade 3 and above could easily read it themselves.

❖ Canadians and Their Government (Canadian Heritage) – This government publication is a free resource available from the government, explaining how our system of government works. To order, contact:

> E-mail: CSP-PEC@pch.gc.ca
> Fax: (613) 998-9008
> Telephone: (613) 998-9030
> Toll Free: 1-877-392-4243

❖ Government: Participating in Canada (by Don Quinlan) – A very easy to read format, this book could be used for almost any age, although best for upper elementary and high school. Gives information about elections, political parties, government in general, law, and citizenship.

❖ Canada Votes! (by Linda Granfield) - A reasonably priced resource about the Canadian electoral process.

❖ Exploring Canada's Electoral System – A cd-rom which explains all aspects of the electoral system in a computer game format. Even the youngest student will enjoy learning about the system, then following the campaign trail, answering questions along the way. A great way for the younger student to begin to understand this process! It is free from the Canadian government. To order, go to **www.tinyurl.com/2149b**.

❖ The Book of Rule: How the World is Governed (Dorling Kindersley Limited) – This beautiful book explains the various methods of government used throughout the world. It is organized by systems of rule (Monarchal, Theocratic, Democratic, etc.) and within each system, by country. For each country this book lists various facts (religion, languages, economics, conflicts, etc.), explains the nature of the government, and notes various issues and challenges the country has faced. Some entries contain pictures and information on various historical leaders. The book is well laid out, and very accessible for the younger high school or even middle school student, while still holding enough information for the older student. Studying the various systems of government throughout the world would add an interesting dimension to the study of Canadian Government.

Planning Form

Unit: 9/3 WWII Date:	Primary (ages 5-9)	Middle (ages 8-12)
Core Reading - Canada	My First History of Canada Ch. 20, parts 6-8	Spotlight Canada Ch. 12-19
Core Reading - World	The Story of the World, Vol. 4 Ch. 27-30	The Story of the World, Vol. 4 Ch. 27-30
Atlas		CH Atlas of Canada Plate 42 World Atlas of the Past pg. 32-39
Videos		
Additional Reading - Non Fiction	*The Spirit of Canada - High Flight p. 196 *Kids' Book of Canadian History p. 56 *Kids' Book of Canadian PM's p. 25-31	*Ultra Hush-hush: Espionage and Special Missions (Shapiro, Stephen) *The Spirit of Canada - High Flight p. 196 - This Was My Brother p. 197 - A Child in Prison Camp p. 198 *Canada Through the Decades: The 1940s **Kids' Book of Canadian History p. 56 *Kids' Book of Canadian PM's p. 25-31
Additional Reading - Historical Fiction		*The Underground Reporters (Kacer, Kathy) *Number the Stars (Lowry, Lois)
Biographies		
Web Sites	www.warmuseum.ca/cwm/cwme.asp www.2learn.ca/mapset/Enjoy/Remember/Re WW2.html www.aviation.technomuses.ca/	
Projects	Draw a picture based on the poem "High Flight."	Make opposite propaganda posters, one for the Allies and one for the Axis countries.
Field Trips	*Visit War Museum *Visit Aviation Museum	*Visit War Museum *Visit Aviation Museum

Jr. High (ages 11-15)	Sr. High (ages 14-19)
A Short History Pt. 4, Ch. 1	A Short History Pt. 4, Ch. 1
The Story of the World, Vol. 4 Ch. 27-30 Young People's Story - Modern World, WW II and Allied Victories	The Story of the World, Vol. 4 Ch. 27-30 Young People's Story - Modern World, WW II and Allied Victories
CH Atlas of Canada Plate 42 World Atlas of the Past pg. 32-39	CH Atlas of Canada Plate 42 World Atlas of the Past pg. 32-39
Canada: A People's History Episodes 13-14	Canada: A People's History Episodes 13-14
*Dr. Suess Goes to War (Minear, Richard) Editorial Cartoons *World War II - History of Warfare Series (Sharpe, Mike) *The Spirit of Canada - High Flight p. 196 - This Was My Brother p. 197 - A Child in Prison Camp p. 198 *Canada Through the Decades: The 1940s	*Dr. Suess Goes to War (Minear, Richard) Editorial Cartoons *World War II - History of Warfare Series (Sharpe, Mike) *Military History of Canada (Morton) Part V *The Spirit of Canada - High Flight p. 196 - This Was My Brother p. 197 - A Child in Prison Camp p. 198
*Number the Stars (Lowry, Lois) *The Zion Chronicles (Thoene, Bodie)	*The Zion Chronicles (Thoene, Bodie)
*Life of a Nazi Soldier (Cartlidge, Cherese) Invitation to the Classics (Lewis, Faulkner, Bonhoeffer) *The Diary of Anne Frank (Frank, Anne)	*Life of a Nazi Soldier (Cartlidge, Cherese) Invitation to the Classics (Lewis, Faulkner, Bonhoeffer) *The Hiding Place (Ten Boon, Corrie)
www.warmuseum.ca/cwm/cwme.asp www.2learn.ca/mapset/Enjoy/Remember/ReWW2.html www.aviation.technomuses.ca/	
Compare/Contrast the two world wars with respect to one topic as listed.	Trace the history of the Jews before, during and after WWII. How much was this war about Hitler's hatred of the Jews? How did it affect their situation in the world?
*Visit War Museum *Visit Aviation Museum	*Visit War Museum *Visit Aviation Museum

Unit: Date:	Primary (ages 5-9)	Middle (ages 8-12)
Core Reading - Canada		
Core Reading - World		
Atlas		
Videos		
Additional Reading - Non Fiction		
Additional Reading - Historical Fiction		
Biographies		
Web Sites		
Projects		
Field Trips		

Jr. High (ages 11-15)	Sr. High (ages 14-19)

Crossword Review Puzzles

Aboriginal Peoples
Unit 1

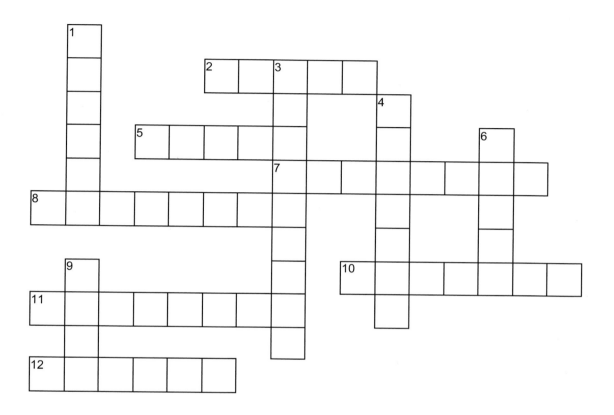

ACROSS

2 Inuit dwelling.
5 Friends of Champlain, enemies of the Iroquois.
7 An aboriginal hero, said to be half god and half man.
8 Pacific coast feast.
10 Plains tribes hunted these.
11 Woodland nation of 5 tribes.
12 Plains dwelling.

DOWN

1 Name meaning "flesh eaters."
3 Woodland dwelling.
4 Tribe encountered in Newfoundland, now extinct.
6 Pacific Coast tribe.
9 Plains tribe.

Aboriginal Peoples
Unit 1 – Challenging

ACROSS

1 This girl was one of the last surviving Beothuk Indians.

6 Tribe encountered in Newfoundland, now extinct.

8 Plains dwelling.

11 Long, narrow boat used by the Inuit.

13 An aboriginal hero, said to be half god and half man.

17 Friends of Champlain, enemies of the Iroquois.

18 The national sport of Canada

19 Woodland dwelling.

20 Large Inuit whaling boat.

21 Northern trail Indians developed these to aid in winter travel.

DOWN

2 Inuit dwelling.

3 Plains tribe.

4 Plains tribes hunted these.

5 Pacific coast feast.

7 Pacific Coast tribe.

9 Some native peoples crossed over from Europe on this.

10 An important community dinner held by the coastal Indians.

12 Beothuk dwelling.

14 Woodland nation of 5 tribes.

15 Native groups of North America are traditionally classified by this many language groups.

16 Name meaning "flesh eaters."

A Meeting of Cultures
Unit 2

ACROSS

1 Name the vikings gave to their North American settlement.
3 Explorer looking for the northern passage. A straight was named after him.
7 Explorer who first landed in North America in 1534.
11 Famous viking explorer.
14 "Canada" means this in the native tongue.
17 One characteristic of the pelts which made them good for hats, was that they were _____.
18 The site of the remains of a viking settlement in eastern Canada.
19 Name of the last Beothuk girl.

DOWN

2 Cabot's real nationality.
4 Country Cartier sailed from.
5 Europeans began trading goods for the pelts of these animals.
6 The first men to stay in Canada (though not year-round) were _____.
8 Explorer who first landed in North America in 1497.
9 Explorer in the north after whom a large bay was named.
10 Navigational instrument used by the early explorers.
12 Country Cabot sailed from.
13 Native chief Cartier met.
15 Native village on the site where Quebec City now stands.
16 The name of Cabot's ship.

Champlain and Beaver Pelts
Unit 3

ACROSS

2 Region of New France on the Atlantic Coast.

4 Men who paddled far up the river to trade for furs from the natives.

7 Champlain named his first cluster of buildings the _____ .

8 In 1710 the _____ conquered Acadia.

10 Young girl who defended her home against the Iroquois.

11 British General who fought against Montcalm for Quebec.

12 Upon seeing Canada, Champlain said, "You could hardly hope to find a more _____ country."

13 French soldiers were given tracts of lands called _____.

DOWN

1 The British fought Montcalm's soldiers on the Plains of _____.

3 Governor General who fought for Quebec.

5 Jesuit Priest who loved the Huron people.

6 Voyageur who lived among the Huron people.

7 People who lived in New France.

9 The name of the mission established by Paul de Maisonneuve.

Settling the Colony
Unit 4

ACROSS

2 Newspaper man in Upper Canada who led a rebellion against the government.
4 Those who wanted to remain under British Rule.
7 Americans who wanted all of North America to be American.
9 Legendary lumberjack.
10 French Canada's leader in the assembly was Louis-Joseph _____.
12 Island in the St. Laurence River where immigrants were held before being allowed into Canada.
13 This colonel and his men built the Rideau Canal.
14 Susanna _____ wrote about living in the bush in Canada.
15 _____ government means the country is run by the people's elected representatives.
16 The War of 1812 ended in eighteen-_____.

DOWN

1 Canada's first Lieutenant-Governor.
3 Former name of Ottawa.
5 General of the British army defending Canada from the Americans in the War of 1812.
6 She chose Ottawa as the home for new Canadian Assembly.
8 Native war chief who helped the Canadians in the War of 1812.
9 Canadians won the victory in the War of 1812 on this man's farm.
10 French Canadian party led by 10 Across.
11 American city which surrendered to the Canadians.

Moving Westward
to Mountains and Oceans
Units 5 & 6

ACROSS

2 The "people in between" of both French and Native.

6 Nickname for James Douglas, governor of Vancouver Island and later of British Columbia.

9 David _____ was a mapmaker who charted much of the western continent.

10 Nickname of Jack Deighton, hotel owner in Vancouver.

11 People chased this commodity from California all the way to the Yukon.

12 Man who came from England to take charge of the Hudson's Bay Company.

DOWN

1 First capital of the colony of British Columbia.

3 Fur trading company who fought with the Nor'Westers for territory.

4 Aristocrat who built a colony for poor Scottish Immigrants at Red River.

5 Plains Indians hunted these.

7 Coastal indians carved these to honour spirits.

8 Alexander _____ came "from Canada by land" in 1793.

Confederation
Unit 7

ACROSS

3 Metis leader who led the Red River uprising.

4 City where the idea of confederation was born.

6 The route escaping slaves took to freedom in Canada is called the _____ railroad.

8 The word "Kanata" which our word "Canada" comes from, means _____.

9 The last province to join confederation in 1949.

DOWN

1 Canada's capital city.

2 Canada became a country on July 1 of eighteen_____.

5 Canada's first Prime Minister.

7 First method of transportation from the east to British Columbia.

Confederation
Unit 7 – Challenging

ACROSS

5 Province that joined confederation on July 20, 1871.
8 Province that joined confederation on July 15, 1870.
10 One of the provinces that joined confederation on September 1, 1905.
12 Number of provinces originally part of confederation.
14 Newspaper man and opponent of John A. Macdonald.
15 One of the provinces that joined confederation on September 1, 1905.
16 Word in the name of our country that was taken from the Bible. The _____ of Canada.
17 The second confederation conference was held here.
18 Province that joined confederation on July 1, 1873.

DOWN

1 Town where the last spike was driven into the Canadian Pacific Railway.
2 Confederation happened in eighteen_____.
3 In 1879 an organized hockey game used a _____ for the first time.
4 Group of Irish who attacked Canada to rebel against Britain.
6 City where the idea of confederation was born.
7 Agnes Macdonald sat on a chair, mounted on the _____ for her first train ride.
9 Province that joined confederation on March 31, 1949.
11 Metis leader in Red River.
13 The route used by escaping slaves to freedom in Canada was called the _____ railroad.

Laurier's Sunny Ways
Unit 8

ACROSS

3 In January, 1901 the well-loved Queen _____ died.

5 Type of wheat developed specifically for growing on the Canadian prairies.

8 Nellie _____ fought for women's rights in Manitoba.

10 French newspaper man who fought against imperialism and Canadian involvement in the Boer War.

11 The _____ brothers flew the first airplane in 1903.

12 Movement to ban alcohol.

DOWN

1 Canadians fought in this war in South Africa.

2 Five women who fought for women's rights were known as the _____.

4 First airplane flown in Canada.

6 People who came from eastern Canada, the US, Britain, and Europe to settle the "last best west."

7 Author of the "Anne of Green Gables" books.

9 The man who invented the radio.

World War I
Unit 9

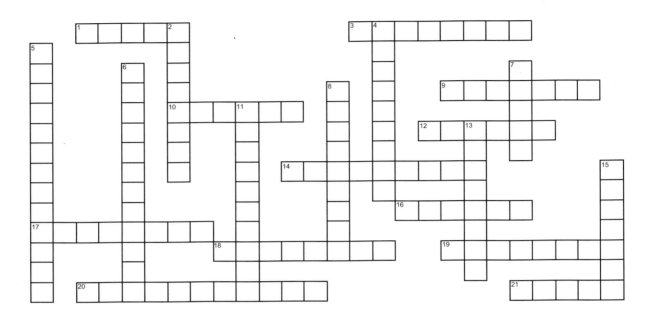

ACROSS

1 We call the German submarines by this name.

3 The armistic of WW I took affect on November _____, 1918.

9 We still wear this flower to honour those who fought in the war.

10 Ships sailing together for protection is called the _____ system.

12 Prime Minister during WW I.

14 WW I began when Archduke _____ was assassinated.

16 The land between the two fronts is called _____ land.

17 Before the war Germany, Italy and Austria-Hungary formed the Triple _____.

18 A famous Canadian poem remembers this field where soldiers were buried.

19 Canadian who shot down von Richthofen.

20 One of the top 3 Allied air aces, this pilot was awarded the Victoria Cross.

21 Battle with record casualties, which earned Canadians the role of "storm troops."

DOWN

2 Much of the war was fought by soldiers in _____.

4 The sinking of this ship helped bring the United States into the war.

5 Place where many soldiers drowned in the mud.

6 Type of aircraft flown by the Allies.

7 Poison gas was used for the first time in the battle of _____.

8 Canadian soldiers' most celebrated victory. Four Canadians won the Victoria Cross in this battle.

11 The peace treaty to end WW I was signed here.

13 German flying ace, von Richthofen, was known as this.

15 Before the war France, Britain and Russia formed the Triple _____.

The Roaring Twenties
And Dirty Thirties
Unit 9

ACROSS

2 This group of artists defined Canadian art of their time.

5 The name given to women who dressed outrageously.

9 The day of the big stock market crash, on October 29, 1929, is known by this nick name.

10 A widespread and serious economic downswing.

13 A Canadian movie star of the 1920s, Mary _____.

17 In 1924 this was discovered in Turner Valley, beginning a boom for Alberta.

19 Became Prime Minister in 1920.

20 Automobiles pulled by horses.

21 A dance craze of the era.

22 The Saskatchewan government paid children a penny for each of these that they turned in.

DOWN

1 Prime Minister during the 1930s.

3 She is a famous Canadian painter from the west.

4 First films with sound.

6 The "Canadian Al Capone."

7 The prairies prospered by growing and selling this product.

8 Maker of the "Model T," making cars accessible to citizens.

11 The occupation of former war pilots who flew from place to place giving air shows.

12 The law banning alcohol.

14 Independent countries with a common allegiance to Britain.

15 Those who brought alcohol into Canada illegally.

16 First woman judge.

18 Prime Minister from 1921-1930.

World War II
Unit 9

ACROSS

2 German leader during WW II.
4 Dictator of Italy during this time.
6 Beach in Normandy where allied forces launched a massive, but unsuccessful, attack.
8 In 1941 Japan attacked this naval base, bringing the United States into the war.
10 German air force.
12 June 6, 1944.
13 Prime Minister of Britain during WW II.
15 After WW I Germany experienced severe economic and political _____.
17 The farthest point of German advance in the Soviet Union.
18 "Lightning Warfare" - Germany's new style of warfare.
20 Hitler was this type of leader.
21 Prime Minister during WW II.
23 Air battle fought over the English Channel.
24 The _____ Act gave parliament the power to make any decisions during wartime without debate.

DOWN

1 Nazi Germany was a _____ state because everything was controlled by the government.
3 Treaty between Germany and Italy.
5 May 8, 1945.
7 Information or ideas spread in order to make people think or feel a certain way.
9 Controversial issue that caused division between English and French Canada during the war.
11 City where the US dropped the first atomic bomb.
14 City where the US dropped the second atomic bomb.
16 Canada entered the war in September of nineteen-_____.
19 Britain and France gave Sudetenland to German in the _____ Agreement in hopes of preventing war.
22 Anti-Semitism is hatred and persecution of the _____.

The Fabulous Fifties
Unit 10

ACROSS

2 Organization created in 1945 to maintain peace between countries.

7 The "King" of rock 'n' roll in the 1950s.

9 Prime Minister from 1957-1963.

11 Production was suddenly shut down on this innovative aircraft.

12 Oil was found once again in Alberta near this city.

13 Canadians of the "Princess Pats" fought bravely at the battle of _____ in Korea.

15 The Dutch royal family sent these to Ottawa to thank Canadians for refuge during WW II.

16 Russian who exposed a spy ring in Ottawa.

17 Instead of building a new airplane, these were purchased for defence .

18 The Korean War began in nineteen_____.

19 American program to give aid to European Countries recovering from the war.

DOWN

1 This province joined confederation in 1949.

3 The race between nations to amass the most weapons.

4 Prime Minister from 1948-1957.

5 An actual structure separating the Communist eastern and western parts of a German city.

6 Major construction project that allowed ocean-going vessels access to the Great Lakes.

8 Imaginary wall separating the Communist countries from the Democratic countries.

10 Treaty signed by 12 countries in 1949.

14 The conflict between the USSR and the Allies in which no shot was fired.

The Swinging Sixties & Seventies
Unit 10

ACROSS

3 Prime Minister from 1963 to 1968.

8 Prime Minister from 1968-1979 and 1980-1984.

9 Canada celebrated her first centennial in nineteen-_____.

11 Prime Minister from 1979-1980.

12 The process in which all Canadian citizens can vote on a particular issue.

15 British trade commissioner who was kidnapped by the FLQ in 1970.

16 Young people who rebelled against society were known as these.

17 The desire of the French for independence is known as this.

18 Expo 67, the 1967 world's fair, was held in this city.

DOWN

1 Quebec Labour Minister who was kidnapped by the FLQ in 1970.

2 The desire of a province to break away from the rest of Canada.

4 New federal political party which began in 1961 by Tommy Douglas.

5 In 1965 Canada got a new _____.

6 Young athlete who quickly earned the title "The Great One," began his hockey career with the Edmonton Oilers in 1976.

7 He scored the winning goal against the USSR in the Canada Cup hockey tournament.

10 Quebec politician who proposed "sovereignty" for Quebec.

13 Popular musical group from Britain.

14 Controversial French president who said "Vive le Quebec Libre!"

The 1980s, 1990s and Beyond!
Unit 10

ACROSS

5 First Canadian woman in space. (1992)

6 Wheelchair athlete who raised money for spinal-cord research in his "Man in Motion" world tour.

7 World Champion figure skater in 1993.

10 Conflict between Iraq and Kuwait in 1990-1991.

12 This attempt to unite French and English Canada failed in 1987.

16 Second trade agreement, signed in 1994, which includes Canada, the United States, and Mexico.

17 State of parliament when fewer than half the seats are held by the governing party.

19 His goal was to run from the Atlantic coast to the Pacific to raise money for cancer research in his "Marathon of Hope" in 1980. He died before he could finish.

20 Prime Minister from 1984-1993.

21 Prime Minister from 1993-2003.

DOWN

1 Agreement, passed in 1989, between Canada and the US for tariff-free trading.

2 Location of an armed conflict between the Mohawks and the army.

3 Location of the Expo 86 world's fair.

4 New name for the British North America Act.

8 First Canadian in space. (1984)

9 Prime Minister from June - September, 1984.

11 First female Prime Minister. She held office from June to November 1993.

13 Movie title used to describe the initiative to remain allies with The United States in both trade and defence.

14 In 1982 she became the first woman governor general of Canada.

15 Canadian-made machine for releasing, rescuing, and repairing satellites. It made its first flight in 1981.

16 Terrorist attack on the World Trade Centre in 2001 is often referred to as this.

17 Prime Minister from 2003-2006.

18 Prime Minister from 2006 - present.

Prime Minister Challenge

See if you can match up the Prime Ministers with the dates they held the PM office. (Hint: Just put them in order.)

1867 – 73; 1878 – 91	Sir Mackenzie Bowell
1873 – 1878	Charles Joseph Clark
1891 – 1892	William Lyon Mackenzie King
1892 – 1894	Pierre Elliott Trudeau
1894 – 1896	Joseph Jacques Jean Chretien
1896	Sir Robert Laird Borden
1896 – 1911	Sir Charles Tupper
1911 – 1920	Avril Kim Campbell
1920 – 1921; 1926	Martin Brian Mulroney
1921 – 1926; 1926 – 1930; 1935 – 1948	John George Diefenbaker
1930 – 1935	Sir Wilfrid Laurier
1948 – 1957	Louis Stephen St. Laurent
1957 – 1963	Sir John Joseph Caldwell Abbott
1963 – 1968	Paul Martin
1968 – 1979; 1980 – 1984	Sir John A. MacDonald
1979 – 1980	Stephen Harper
1984 – 1984	John Napier Turner
1984 – 1993	Arthur Meighen
1993	Sir John Sparrow David Thompson
1993 – 2003	Lester Bowles Pearson
2003 – 2006	Richard Bedford Bennett
2006 –	Alexander Mackenzie

Crossword Puzzle Solutions

Aboriginal Peoples
Unit 1

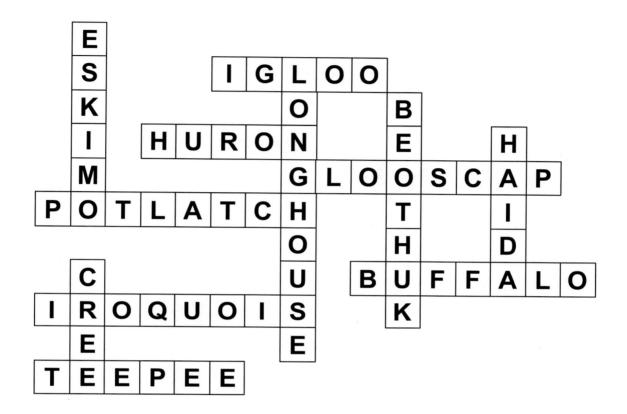

Aboriginal Peoples
Unit 1 – Challenging

A Meeting of Cultures
Unit 2

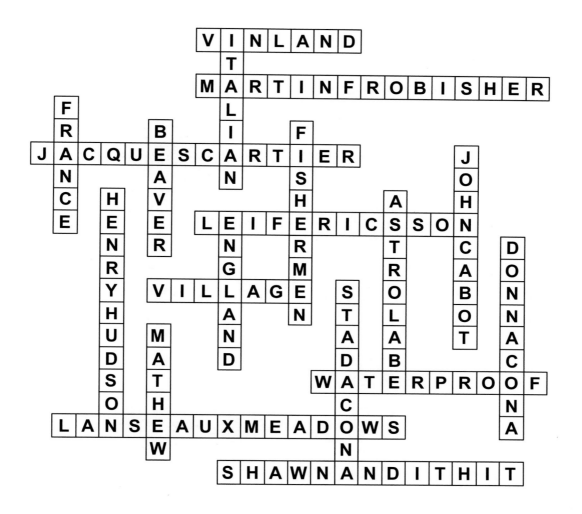

Champlain and Beaver Pelts
Unit 3

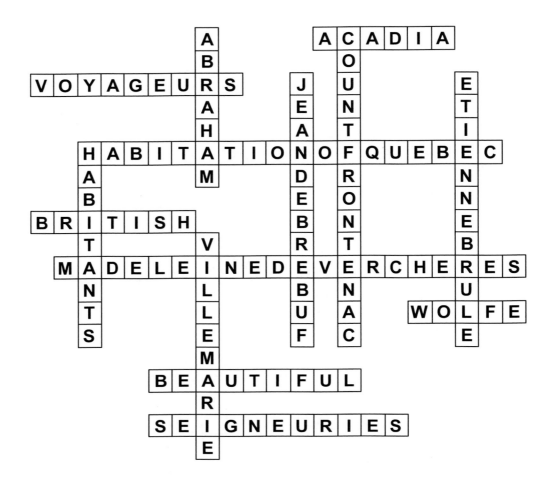

Settling the Colony
Unit 4

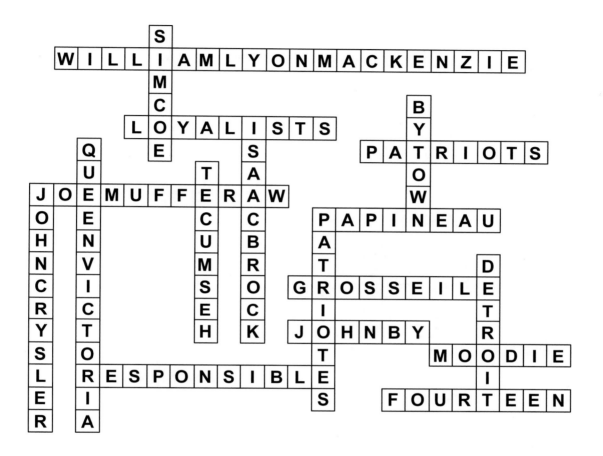

Moving Westward
to Mountains and Oceans
Units 5 & 6

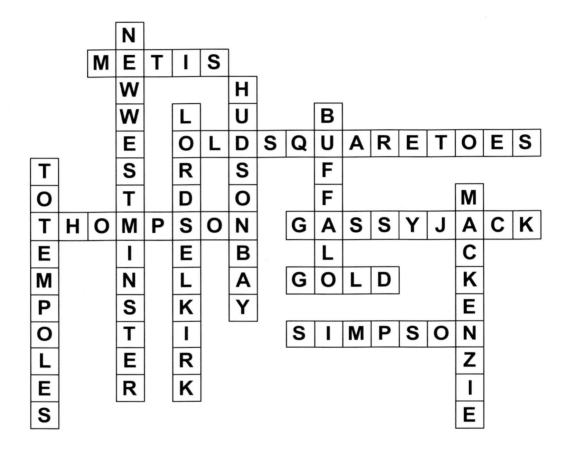

Confederation
Unit 7

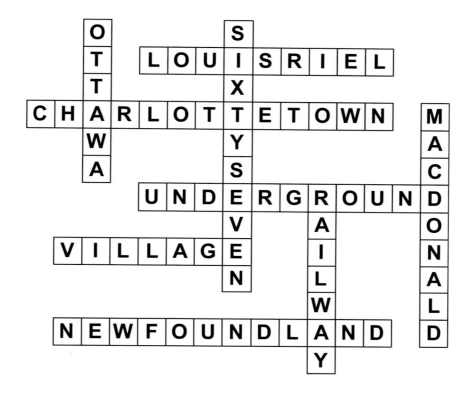

Confederation
Unit 7 – Challenging

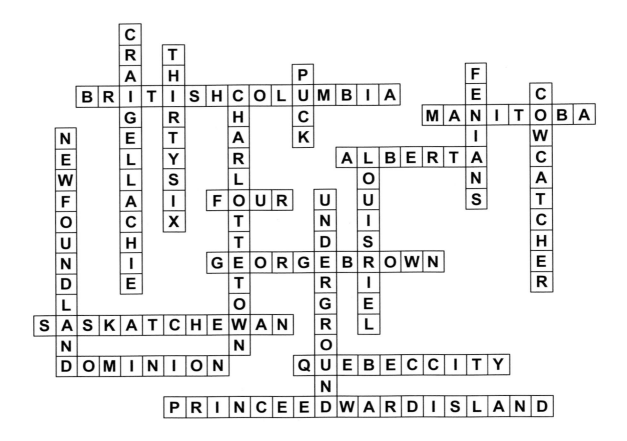

Laurier's Sunny Ways
Unit 8

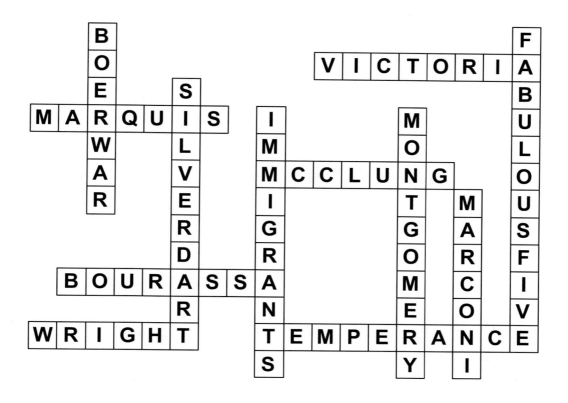

World War I
Unit 9

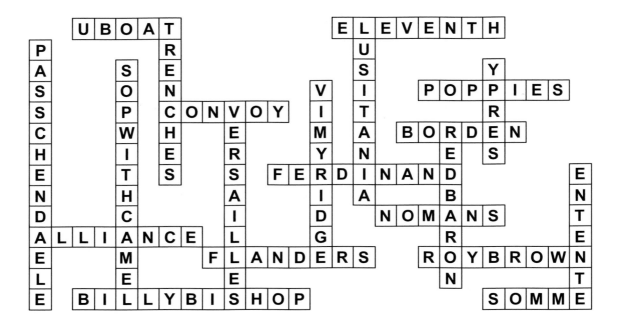

The Roaring Twenties
And Dirty Thirties
Unit 9

World War II
Unit 9

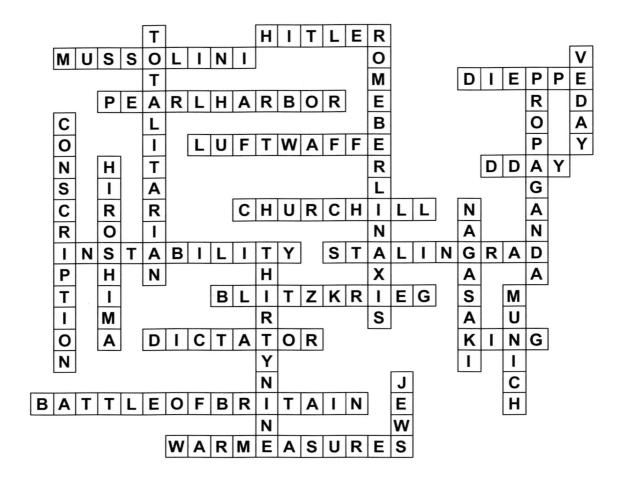

The Fabulous Fifties
Unit 10

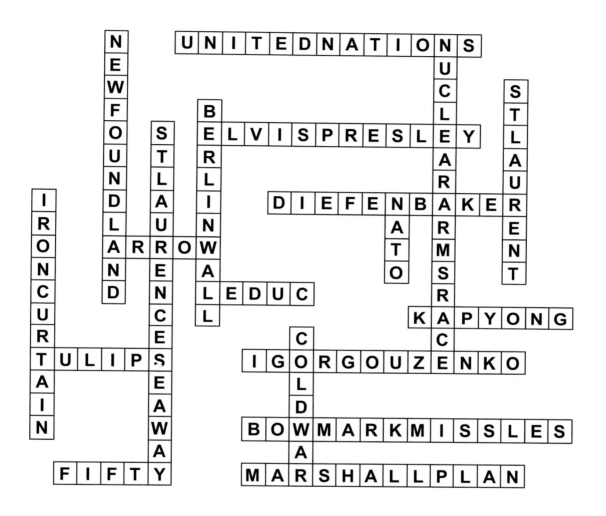

The Swinging Sixties & Seventies
Unit 10

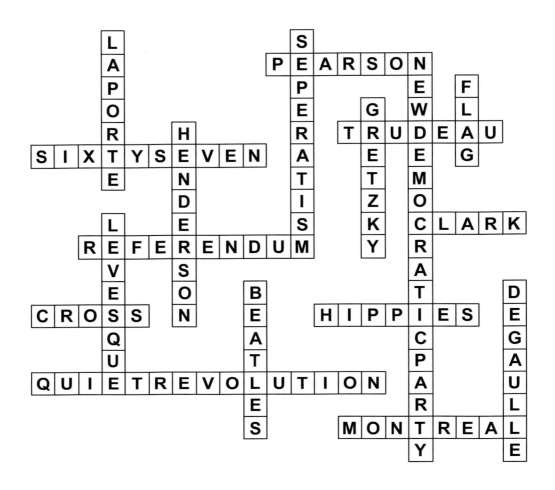

The 1980s, 1990s & Beyond!
Unit 10

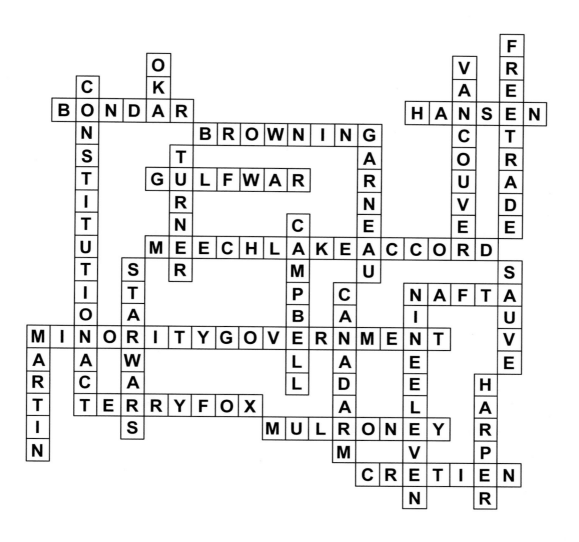

Prime Minister Challenge

1867– 73; 1878-91…………………………	Sir John A. MacDonald
1873 – 1878………………………..…….	Alexander Mackenzie
1891 – 1892………………………….…	Sir John Joseph Caldwell Abbott
1892 – 1894……………………………..	Sir John Sparrow David Thompson
1894 – 1896……………………………..	Sir Mackenzie Bowell
1896……………………………………..	Sir Charles Tupper
1896 – 1911…………………..………...	Sir Wilfrid Laurier
1911 – 1920……………………………...	Sir Robert Laird Borden
1920 – 1921; 1926………………………...	Arthur Meighen
1921 – 1926; 1926 – 1930; 1935 – 1948 ...	William Lyon Mackenzie King
1930 – 1935…………………………….…	Richard Bedford Bennett
1948 – 1957……………………………..	Louis Stephen St. Laurent
1957 – 1963……………………...............	John George Diefenbaker
1963 – 1968……………………...............	Lester Bowles Pearson
1968 – 1979; 1980 – 1984……………..…...	Pierre Elliott Trudeau
1979 – 1980……………………………..	Charles Joseph Clark
1984 – 1984……………………………..	John Napier Turner
1984 – 1993……………………………..	Martin Brian Mulroney
1993…………………………………..	Avril Kim Campbell
1993 – 2003……………………...............	Joseph Jacques Jean Chretien
2003 – 2006……………………………..	Paul Martin
2006 – ………………………………..	Stephen Harper

Manufactured by Amazon.ca
Acheson, AB

11145183R00103